THE INSTANT POT® ULTIMATE
SOUS VIDE COOKBOOK

THE INSTANT POT® ULTIMATE
SOUS VIDE COOKBOOK

100 NO-PRESSURE RECIPES
FOR PERFECT MEALS EVERY TIME

JASON LOGSDON

STERLING EPICURE
New York

To Jodi

THANKS FOR BEING THE BEST FRIEND, PARTNER,
AND WIFEY A GUY COULD EVER ASK FOR.

STERLING EPICURE
New York

An Imprint of Sterling Publishing Co., Inc.
1166 Avenue of the Americas
New York, NY 10036

ISBN 978-1-4549-3316-8

Distributed in Canada by Sterling Publishing Co., Inc.
C/o Canadian Manda Group, 664 Annette Street
Toronto, Ontario M6S 2C8, Canada
Distributed in the United Kingdom by GMC Distribution Services
Castle Place, 166 High Street, Lewes, East Sussex BN7 1XU, England
Distributed in Australia by NewSouth Books
45 Beach Street, Coogee, NSW 2034, Australia

For information about custom editions, special sales,
and premium and corporate purchases, please contact
Sterling Special Sales at 800-805-5489 or specialsales@sterlingpublishing.com.

Manufactured in Canada

2 4 6 8 10 9 7 5 3 1

sterlingpublishing.com

Cover design by Elizabeth Mihaltse Lindy
Interior design by Matchbook Digital
For Image credits, please see page 169.

Contents

DISCARDED

Sous Vide Overview

Sous vide can be intimidating when you approach it for the first time, but once you understand a few key concepts you realize how easy it is to use. Whether you are looking to make convenient everyday meals that taste great, or you want to up your gourmet game and seriously impress your friends and family, sous vide is an amazing tool to have in your cooking toolbox.

Just Getting Started?

Trying to decide how much information to include about sous vide is always a tough decision for me. I don't want to leave new people out in the cold and confused about how sous vide works, but I also don't want to fill up space that experienced sous viders will skip over.

As a compromise, this book offers a brief overview of how sous vide works and then provides links to my free online articles that examine these topics in greater detail. That way the novice sous vide cook can get up to speed while the experts can jump right to the recipes. So keep an eye out for the Notes blocks that will have links to more information.

And if you are really unsure about how sous vide works, I recommend my free email course, which will walk you through the entire process from start to finish at AFMEasy.com/SExplore.

Sous Vide Steps

When sous viding food, you almost always follow the same process.

The first step is to trim and season your food, just as you normally do in traditional cooking. Many of the same seasonings can be used, including spice rubs and most herbs. I usually salt my food before sous viding it, though many people omit that step for longer cooking times. The only big difference is that aromatics, like raw garlic and onion, are usually not used because they will not break down with the lower temperatures used in sous vide.

The second step is to determine the time and temperature at which you want to cook your food. If you are following a recipe, this information should be provided. If you are cooking something without a recipe, you can use the charts starting on page 151 to figure it out for other foods.

The third step is to enclose your food to protect it during the sous vide process. This is usually done by sealing it in plastic sous vide bags, but some recipes use canning jars or other vessels. Most of the sealing is done using a vacuum sealer or Ziploc Brand® freezer bags.

Fourth, you place the bags in a water bath that is held to the specific temperature you decided on and let them cook for a set amount of time.

Finally, once the food is cooked, you remove it from the water bath and the bag, and normally finish it off by searing. Once you've gone through the process a handful of times, it'll become second nature to you! The food coming out of the sous vide water bath can be very hot, especially for food cooked to a high temperature. *Always handle hot foods carefully. It is usually best to handle the bags and food like you would any type of heated food, by using tongs, spatulas, and even oven mitts when needed.*

Sous Vide Safety

Before moving into other areas of the sous vide process, I want to talk about sous vide safety. The main areas we will look at are the Danger Zone, Temperature versus Time, and Plastic Safety.

Keep in mind that sous vide is no more or less safe than other methods of cooking. There's a lot of talk about the danger of cooking food sous vide, but it's just as easy to make yourself sick by undercooking a chicken in the oven or undercooking grilled pork. So don't be intimidated: Once you know a few rules of thumb, you'll be all set. And what you learn for sous vide can also be applied to make all your cooking safer.

DANGER ZONE

If there is one takeaway about food safety, it is understanding the danger zone.

The bacteria we are trying to remove during cooking thrive from around 40°F (4.4°C) to 126°F (52.2°C). They stop growing, but don't start dying quickly, until around 130°F (54.4°C). That range between 40°F (4.4°C) and 126°F (52.2°C) is known as the "danger zone" (cue Top Gun music) and it's often referred to in food safety circles.

The longer food is held in the danger zone, the more likely you are to get sick from it. Most government agencies suggest that anything less than 4 hours is safe. Longer than that, it depends on what your tolerance for risk is, and whether or not you are serving it to people with immunodeficiencies.

TEMPERATURE VERSUS TIME

When people start with sous vide, they are often confused as to why it is suddenly okay to cook chicken or pork to an internal temperature of 140°F (60°C), when traditionally it has to be cooked to a much higher temperature.

We have always been taught that temperature is what makes food safe, but that's only half the equation. What makes food safe is actually a combination of the temperature it is heated to and the length of time it is held at that temperature. That time and temperature combine to pasteurize the food, making it safe to eat.

A piece of chicken heated to 140°F (60°C) and held there for 30 minutes is actually just as safe as one heated to 165°F (73.9°C) for 1 second. The reason the government suggests such a high temperature is that the pathogens are killed instantly at that temperature, but the same levels of pasteurization occur at much lower temperatures over longer periods. Using sous vide allows you to take advantage of this, since food cooked to lower temperatures results ends up being much moister.

PLASTIC SAFETY

A main concern of sous vide safety is cooking in plastic and whether or not this is a dangerous practice. Most scientists and chefs believe that cooking in food-safe, BPA-free plastic at these low temperatures does not pose any risk. The temperature is about equivalent to leaving a bottle of water in your car, or in a semi-truck during transport, in the summer. This includes Ziploc freezer bags, sous vide bags, and most food-safe plastics.

However, I find it hard to believe that we know everything about how plastic reacts to heat, water, our bodies, and the environment. As such, I encourage you to read up on the safety of plastic in sous vide and plastic in general and come to your own conclusions about the safety of using these techniques. I hope this will at least give you some varied perspectives on it so you can make an informed opinion of your own.

Note: For more information about sous vide safety, including deep dives into all the topics above, go to AFMEasy.com/SSafe.

Sous Vide Times

The two components that determine how your food will turn out are time and temperature. My recipes give you the time and temperature I recommend, but learning about why I suggest them allows you to tweak the recipes to your own tastes. The length of time you cook your food will accomplish three different things.

HEAT THE FOOD

At the most basic level, cooking is about heating up food. Applying heat to food long enough to heat it through usually results in more tender, flavorful, and better-tasting food. This is usually how we cook steaks and tender vegetables.

With most traditional cooking methods, there is a fine line between heating the food properly and overcooking it. In other words, you need to pull your steak off the grill right when it is done; otherwise, it gets burned. With sous vide, you have complete control over the food, and the timing is much less critical because you are cooking at the temperature you want your food to end up. When you are heating the food through with sous vide, the timing almost always depends just on the thickness of the food.

MAKE THE FOOD SAFE THROUGH PASTEURIZATION

Once the food is heated, we often leave it on the heat to ensure that it is pasteurized and safe to eat.

This is how we traditionally cook chicken, pork, and hamburgers.

Pasteurized food has had the amount of dangerous bacteria and parasites in it reduced to acceptable levels (the US government suggests killing all but 1 in a million, or 1 in 10 million, depending on the pathogen). Pasteurized food is then generally safe to eat, provided it is eaten within a few hours so the remaining bacteria do not have time to regrow. Pasteurization is achieved by holding food at a specific temperature for a certain length of time, with higher temperatures resulting in faster pasteurization.

Many people wonder which foods need to be pasteurized. Some foods, like chicken, almost always must be pasteurized. All foods can be pasteurized, though, and numerous people always pasteurize for added safety. It is also safest to pasteurize all food when cooking for immunocompromised individuals, like the elderly, those with chronic illnesses, and pregnant women.

I note in recipes when I recommend that food should be pasteurized and not just heated through.

TENDERIZE THE FOOD

The final step for some foods, after they are heated through and pasteurized, is to cook them long enough so they become tender. This is critical for many tough cuts of meat, especially those that would traditionally be braised or smoked for long periods.

As food gets hot, the muscle, collagen, and protein undergo transformations that cause the food to get more and more tender. The higher the temperature the food is cooked at, the faster this tenderization occurs. Many sous vide temperatures are very low when compared to traditional cooking methods, which means it takes a longer time, but the lower temperatures result in a much moister end dish. Once temperatures in most meats go above 140°F (60°C) the meat begins to dry out and become blander. Using sous vide, you can hold the meat below 140°F (60°C) for a long enough time for the tenderizing process to run its course.

Note: For more information about sous vide times, read the tables at the back of this book or go to AFMEasy.com/STime.

Sous Vide Temperatures

The most important thing to know when trying to consistently create amazing food with sous vide is understanding how time and temperature interact to cook your food. In the previous section, we talked about how sous vide times work and now we will look at sous vide temperatures.

As opposed to most traditional cooking methods, sous vided food is cooked at the temperature you want the final food to end up at. This is usually between 120°F (48.9°C) and 185°F (85°C), depending on the food being prepared.

As meat is heated, its components change. These changes result in structural transformations that affect the texture, juiciness, and mouth feel of the meat. The higher the temperature applied to the meat, the faster these changes occur.

As proteins are heated, they begin to contract. This contraction squeezes moisture out of the meat, which is one reason well-done steaks are so dry. On the flip side, when collagen is heated, it breaks down, releasing gelatin and resulting in tender meat, which is one reason pot roasts and braises are fall-apart tender. Choosing the right temperature for what you are trying to accomplish is critical to successful cooking.

As meat is heated above 120°F (48.9°C) it starts to get tenderized. The meat also starts to become firmer, but with minimal moisture loss. Above 140°F (60°C) the meat really starts to lose moisture as it contracts, resulting in much firmer, drier meat.

Above 156°F (68.9°C) more moisture is removed from the meat as it clumps together. However, collagen also begins breaking down quickly, adding a lubricating gelatin and creating a "fall-apart" texture.

This breakdown of collagen is why many traditionally cooked tough cuts of meat are braised or roasted for a long period, ensuring that the meat becomes fully tenderized. However, because of the high temperatures, those cuts of meat can easily become dried out.

Using sous vide allows you to hold the meat below the 140°F (60°C) barrier long enough for the slower tenderization process to be effective. This results in very tender meat that is still moist and not overcooked, with a steaklike texture. Sous vide also allows you replicate braise-like texture by cooking tough cuts in the 156°F (68.9°C) to 176°F (80°C) range, which is still much lower than traditional braising temperatures and results in moister meat.

Note: For more information about sous vide temperatures, including a detailed look at how it affects food, go to AFMEasy.com/STemp or check out the charts at the back of this book.

Sous Vide Equipment

To effectively sous vide, there are three main pieces of equipment you need. Each piece of equipment comes in a variety of types and at a range of price points. Here's a brief overview so you can determine what is best for you.

SEALING THE FOOD

The first type of equipment is something to seal the food with. The three main options here are Ziploc Brand freezer bags, a vacuum-edge sealer like a FoodSaver, or a chamber vacuum sealer like a VacMaster.

Note: Ziploc brand freezer bags are inexpensive and work relatively well, especially for cooking times of less than 12 hours. I used them for several years with very few issues. Be sure to use Ziploc brand freezer bags, or another bag rated for use in high temperatures, as many generic bags are not.

Edge sealers cost about $100 and are a great option for people looking to move to a more robust solution than Ziploc bags. Chamber vacuum sealers are the most powerful of the sealers and cost several hundred dollars, but they are worth considering if you regularly seal food for storage anyway.

Note: For more information about sealing food for sous vide, go to AFMEasy.com/SSeal for an in-depth look at sealers as well as reviews of and recommendations for specific machines.

HEATING THE WATER

The second type of equipment is something to heat the water. There are a few main options, but the most popular is a sous vide circulator. These wand-like machines go in a pot of water and heat it to a specific temperature, then maintain that temperature indefinitely. They make sous vide a truly hands-off process, and many can be found for around $100.

For those just getting started, you can also try out sous vide on a stove or even in a beer cooler. These methods are slightly less reliable, and are only practical for shorter cooking times, but they are effective ways to experiment with sous vide without spending any money upfront.

Note: Go to AFMEasy.com/SCirc for an in-depth look at heating options, as well as reviews of and recommendations for specific machines.

SEARING THE FOOD

Searing after sous vide is a critical step for most types of food, especially meat and fish. It adds a level of flavor and complexity that you won't get from sous vide alone. It also makes the food look much more appealing.

There are many ways to sear your food, but the easiest is to pan-fry it. It's the cheapest method since you probably already have a pan and a stove and it's great for people just getting started. Many experienced sous viders rave about using cast-iron pans as their go-to searing tool.

I often use a Bernzomatic™ torch to sear my food. It results in less overcooking and requires minimal cleanup, compared to pan searing. Many people use the Searzall™ attachment for this torch as well.

When I'm looking for more flavor, I'll turn to my grill to sear the food. You just crank it up as hot as possible before putting the food on. You can also reheat food in a smoker to add additional levels of flavor, a process I suggest for the Smoked BBQ Brisket with Grilled Summer Squash and Onions (page 32) and the Smoked Baby Back Ribs (page 56).

For nonuniform foods with lots of nooks and crannies, such as roasts or chicken legs, a broiler can be reasonably effective.

PROPER PAN SEARING TECHNIQUE

Searing is critical for adding flavor and texture to sous vided foods. Make sure you sear your food as quickly as possible to minimize further cooking. Most sears should only take 1 to 2 minutes per side.

The key to a successful sear is to completely dry off your food with paper towels or a clean kitchen cloth before adding it to the pan. Then heat some oil in a pan until it just barely starts to smoke. It's best to use an oil with a high smoke point—like avocado, ghee, extra-light olive oil, or peanut oil—both to get a higher temperature and to help keep your house from becoming filled with smoke. Once the oil is heated and almost smoking, place the food in the pan. After 1 to 2 minutes, flip the food, give it another minute or two, then pull it off the heat. The shorter the time in the pan the better. For foods such as thin steaks or fish fillets I will only sear one side to minimize the overcooking.

If you really want a deep sear, you can also let the food cool down, or place it in an ice bath, before searing it. This will allow you to sear it for longer without overcooking it.

Recipe Notes

I strive to make each individual recipe as clear as possible, but there are some things that apply to all the recipes. **Make sure to read through this section before you start cooking so there will be no confusion!**

Read the Whole Recipe First

Some recipes require curing the food, cooking for 2 days, or other steps that take time. Please read through the entire recipe before starting on it so you know you have the time to make the dish, and you have all the ingredients on hand.

Timing Directions

Many recipes say, "Cook for X hours, at least until heated through" or "Cook for X hours, at least until pasteurized." This refers to the tables starting on page 151, which give you the time needed for the specific piece of meat you are cooking. I do try to give a common range, which you can follow if you don't want to refer to the tables.

Timing Range

Most recipes, and the charts at the back of the book, include a range of time for when the food is done.

For most cuts of meat, it is important to remember that it will be "perfectly" cooked anywhere in that range. It is similar to ordering a steak medium-rare: We don't usually concern ourselves if it is cooked to 131°F (55°C) or 133°F (56.1°C); it will still be great at either temperature, as will a sirloin steak that is sous vided 3 hours or 6 hours.

Note: This is such a counterintuitive point that I have written much longer about it at AFMEasy.com/SRange if you want to gain a deeper understanding.

Salting

For most foods that are cooked, I assume that you are salting and tasting the food as you go. Tasting your food as you cook it is critical, so I recommend that you do it often during the cooking process for proteins as well as for the sides.

Obscure Ingredients

I try to make my recipes as nuanced as possible, but you can usually substitute the following ingredients with very little effect on the final dish:

Vinegars
Chili powders
Finishing salts

Olive oil for oil of your choice

Paprika can be sweet or smoked

Keep in mind that if your local grocery store doesn't stock certain ingredients, you can almost always find them online.

Common Ingredients

There are many ingredients that I assume you have on hand and don't call out specifically in the ingredients list for every recipe. These include:

Olive oil

A searing oil, such as avocado, canola, or grapeseed oil

Salt and pepper

Water

Sealing Foods

All timing assumes that the food is sealed in a single layer in the sous vide bag. If you need to use multiple bags to accomplish this, it is completely fine to use as many bags as you need. This is true both for meat and for fruits and vegetables.

Mixing Up Components

I put together these recipes with specific pairing in mind, but most of the proteins, sides, and sauces can all be used with each other. If the Scallops with Mango Salsa (page 104) sounds tasty but you prefer steak, go for it!

I also hope you will tweak the recipes to meet your needs and tastes, or to the ingredients you have on hand.

Keeping Food Warm

The best way to keep food hot is to serve it on a heated plate. This isn't critical to the success of the dishes here, but it is a helpful tip. I usually turn the oven on low, around 200°F (93.3°C) and let it heat, then turn it off and put the plates in to make sure they don't get too hot. And be sure you use oven-safe plates!

Use a Thicker Cut

Getting a good sear on a thin piece of meat without overcooking it can be very hard. I recommend using a thicker piece, searing it, and then cutting it into serving portions. For instance, instead of using four small sirloin steaks, use one thick one that you can then cut up after searing. It will allow you to get a much better sear without overcooking the meat.

Spice Rub Amounts

To make it easy to measure, I often overestimate the amount of spice rubs that are made (it's hard to measure $\frac{1}{16}$ [0.25ml] of a teaspoon!). So, don't feel like you have to use it all; usually a light coating is best.

Adjusting Recipe Size

Most of the recipes in this book are portioned for four people. You can easily increase or decrease the amount of food you are cooking with very little effort. In contrast to most traditional methods, with sous vide the cooking time and temperature don't change as the amount of food increases, as long as the thickness stays the same. So you can make 10 chicken breasts in just as much time as 2, as long as you have room in your water bath and seal them in a single layer.

Common Temperature Ranges

The recipes here specify the recommended temperatures, and have been tested for optimum results, but you should feel free to use whatever temperature suits your tastes. Here are some of the more common ranges I use when determining what temperature to sous vide food at:

FOOD	INTERNAL TEMPERATURE
Rare beef, lamb, and red meat	120°F–129°F (48.9°C–53.8°C)
Medium-rare beef, lamb, and red meat	130°F–139°F (54.4°C–59.4°C)
Medium beef, lamb, and red meat	140°F–145°F (60°C–62.8°C)
Traditional "braised" beef, lamb, and red meat	156°F–176°F (68.9°C–80°C)
Moist, tender pork	135°F–144°F (57.2°C–62.2°C)
Traditional tender pork	145°F–155°F (62.8°C–68.3°C)
Traditional "braised" pork	156°F–176°F (68.9°C–80°C)
Extra-rare chicken and poultry white meat	136°F–139°F (57.8°C–59.4°C)
Traditional chicken and poultry white meat	140°F–150°F (60°C–65.6°C)
Traditional chicken and poultry dark meat	140°F–150°F (60°C–65.6°C)
Shreddable chicken and poultry dark meat	156°F-176°F (68.9°C–80°C)
Mi-cuit fish	104°F (40°C)
Firm Sashimi	110°F (43.3°C)
Traditional fish	122°F–131°F (50°C–55°C)
Flaky fish	132°F–140°F (55.5°C–60°C)
Fruits and vegetables	180°F–190°F (82.2°C–87.8°C)

Picking a temperature is as easy as figuring out what kind of meat you want and selecting any number in that range. Once you have tried out a few different temperatures, you can get a feel for what you prefer. For instance, I cook all my beef steaks at 131°F (55°C), but if you prefer a medium steak, increase the temperature to 140°F (60°C).

CHAPTER 1

Beef and Lamb

BEEF AND LAMB SOUS VIDE

Beef is the first thing many people turn to when they get their sous vide machines. It is amazing how easy it is to make an incredibly tasty sous vide steak. There are two main ways to prepare beef and red meat—steaklike and braise-like.

STEAKLIKE TEXTURE

Steaklike texture is what you think of as the texture of a rib eye, sirloin, or other piece of steak. With traditional cooking, you can only have steaklike texture from tender cuts, but with sous vide you can make any piece of meat steaklike, including chuck roasts and short ribs.

The temperature used for steaklike texture depends on how you like your steak cooked. The main ranges are:

Rare: 120°F–129°F (48.9°C–53.8°C)
Medium Rare: 130°F–139°F (54.4°C–59.4°C)
Medium: 140°F–145°F (60°C–62.8°C)
Well Done: Above 145°F (62.8°C)

The only exception is that you can't cook tougher cuts for more than a few hours at a temperature below 128°F (53.3°C) because you are still in or near the danger zone.

BRAISELIKE TEXTURE

Braiselike texture characterizes pot roasts, shredded beef, and other "fall off the bone" meats. Many tough cuts, especially those with a lot of fat or connective tissue, can be made braiselike. Almost all braiselike sous viding is done above 150°F (65.6°C), and the three temperatures I recommend starting with are:

156°F (68.9°C) for a shreddable, but still firm texture
165°F (73.9°C) for a more fall-apart texture
176°F (80°C) for a really fall-apart texture

BEEF AND LAMB TIMING

Most tender cuts only need to be heated through, which typically takes 2 to 3 hours. Tough cuts have to be heated long enough to become tenderized, which can take 1 to 3 days, depending on the cut. For cooking times for specific pieces of meat, consult the charts at the back of the book.

OTHER RED MEAT

These recommendations work for beef, lamb, and many other types of red meat. Some of my readers have even discussed cooking moose, elk, bear, kangaroo, and bison. However, if you are eating wild game, you should become aware of the pathogens these game meats may carry and what temperatures are needed to kill them, as it may differ from beef.

RIB EYE WITH CHIPOTLE BUTTER

COOKS: 131°F (55°C) FOR 2 TO 4 HOURS | SERVES: 4

I love to eat rib eye and I usually don't cook it with anything besides salt and pepper, but sometimes I like to add a little kick for variety. This spicy chipotle butter not only packs a punch when slathered on a steak, but also adds richness and flavor.

I often pair the chipotle butter with some refreshing coleslaw. It helps tone down the heat and adds a crispy texture.

FOR THE RIB EYE

1 teaspoon (5ml) garlic powder

½ teaspoon (2.5ml) smoked paprika

½ teaspoon (2.5ml) ancho pepper powder

1–2 pounds (450–900g) rib-eye steak

FOR THE CHIPOTLE BUTTER

¼ cup (60ml) butter, softened at room temperature

¼–1 teaspoon (1–5ml) minced chipotle peppers in adobo sauce

½ teaspoon (2.5ml) paprika

⅛ teaspoon (0.5ml) freshly cracked black pepper

FOR THE COLESLAW

1½ cups (355ml) shredded cabbage

1 cup (237ml) shredded carrots

3 tablespoons (45ml) mayonnaise

2 tablespoons (30ml) mustard, preferably whole grain

2 tablespoons (30ml) olive oil

TO ASSEMBLE

2 tablespoons (30ml) chopped fresh oregano leaves

Sea salt

For the Rib Eye

Preheat a water bath to 131°F (55°C).

Mix together the spices in a small bowl. Lightly salt and pepper the rib eye, then sprinkle with the spices. Place the steak in a sous vide bag and seal. Place the bag in the water bath and cook for 2 to 4 hours, until heated through.

For the Chipotle Butter

Place all the butter ingredients in a bowl and mix and mash thoroughly, using a fork.

For the Coleslaw

Place all the ingredients in a bowl and mix until thoroughly combined. Season with salt and pepper.

To Assemble

Take the sous vide bag out of the water and remove the cooked rib-eye steak. Dry it off thoroughly, using paper towels or a clean dish cloth. Lightly salt the steak, then quickly sear it for 1 to 2 minutes per side, just until browned, then remove from the heat. Cut into serving portions.

Place the rib eye on a plate and top with some of the chipotle butter. Place the coleslaw next to it and sprinkle everything with the oregano leaves and sea salt, then serve.

FILET MIGNON WITH COGNAC CREAM SAUCE

COOKS: 131°F (55°C) FOR 2 TO 4 HOURS | SERVES: 4

When my family goes out to a steakhouse, my dad always orders filet mignon, also called beef tenderloin. He loves how tender and lean it is. The downside to this lack of fat, especially the lack of marbling, is a reduction in flavor. This is why filet mignon is often served with a sauce of some kind. There are many options for sauces, but this cognac cream sauce is one of my favorites. It fills the meal with bold flavors.

Because it is so tender, filet mignon is less forgiving than most types of meat. Once it is heated through, it should be removed from the water fairly quickly.

FOR THE FILET MIGNON

1–2 pounds (450–900g) filet mignon steak

TO ASSEMBLE

4 tablespoons (60ml) butter

2 shallots, sliced

1 cup (237ml) heavy cream

½ cup (118ml) cognac

2 teaspoons (10ml) Dijon mustard

2 teaspoons (10ml) Worcestershire sauce

For the Filet Mignon

Preheat a water bath to 131°F (55°C).

Lightly salt and pepper the steak, then place it in a sous vide bag and seal. Place the bag in the water bath and cook for 2 to 4 hours, until heated through.

To Assemble

Heat a pan over medium-high to high heat.

Take the sous vide bag out of the water and remove the cooked filet mignon steak. Dry it off thoroughly, using paper towels or a clean dish cloth. Lightly salt and pepper the steak. Quickly sear it for 1 to 2 minutes per side, just until browned, then remove from the heat.

Turn the pan down to medium, add the butter, and let it melt. Add the shallots and cook until softened. Add the heavy cream then the cognac, being careful of flare-ups, and cook until reduced slightly and the alcohol has cooked off. Add the Dijon mustard and Worcestershire sauce, then stir to combine. Bring to a simmer, then remove the sauce from the heat. To serve, pour it over the steak.

> TIP The cognac fumes can ignite during the sauce preparation, especially if you have a gas stove, so it is wise to deliberately ignite them regularly to prevent a bigger flare-up when you aren't expecting it.

SIRLOIN STEAK TACOS WITH CORN AND AVOCADO SALSA

COOKS: 131°F (55°C) FOR 2 TO 4 HOURS, OR UP TO 10 HOURS | SERVES: 4

My wife is a big fan of tacos, and I've been trying to cook them more regularly for her. This is a super-quick recipe that I can pull out on a weeknight for a fast but flavor-packed meal. The salsa comes together quickly and the sirloin steak is very tender after sous viding for 10 hours, which is perfect if you are at work all day.

These tacos can are even great with pulled pork or chicken strips. You can also serve these with any traditional Tex-Mex toppings, like sour cream, refried beans, and rice.

FOR THE SIRLOIN STEAK

½ teaspoon (2.5ml) garlic powder

¼ teaspoon (1ml) dried oregano

1–2 pounds (450–900g) sirloin steak

FOR THE CORN AND AVOCADO SALSA

1 cup (237ml) cooked corn kernels

2 tomatoes, diced

1 avocado, diced

½ cup (118ml) black beans, either canned or cooked

2 tablespoons (30ml) chopped red onion

¼ cup (60ml) chopped fresh cilantro

4 cloves garlic, diced

2 tablespoons (30ml) olive oil

1 teaspoon (5ml) fresh lime juice

TO ASSEMBLE

8 soft corn tortillas

For the Sirloin Steak

Preheat a water bath to 131°F (55°C).

Mix together the spices in a small bowl. Lightly salt and pepper the sirloin steak, then sprinkle with the spices. Place the meat in a sous vide bag and seal. Place the bag in the water bath and cook for 2 to 4 hours, until heated through, or up to 10 hours, until tenderized.

For the Corn and Avocado Salsa

Combine all the ingredients in a bowl and mix well.

To Assemble

Take the sous vide bag out of the water and remove the cooked sirloin steak. Dry it off thoroughly, using paper towels or a clean dish cloth. Lightly salt the steak then quickly sear it for 1 to 2 minutes per side, just until browned, then remove from the heat. Cut the sirloin steak into slices.

Add some sirloin steak strips to a tortilla, top with the corn and avocado salsa, then serve.

STRIP STEAK WITH ROASTED BRUSSELS SPROUTS

COOKS: 131°F (55°C) FOR 2 TO 4 HOURS | SERVES: 4

Brussels sprouts are delicious, whether shredded in salads, sautéed with bacon, or, as in this recipe, simply roasted with cherry tomatoes and garlic. They should be cooked until they soften, but still have a little firmness to them.

I like to serve this meal family-style because it makes such a nice presentation, but, if you want to plate the meal individually, you can cut the steak into strips.

FOR THE STRIP STEAK

1–2 pounds (450–900g) strip steak

FOR THE ROASTED BRUSSELS SPROUTS

2 pounds (900g) Brussels sprouts
4 cloves garlic, minced
2 tablespoons (30ml) olive oil
1 pint (473ml) cherry tomatoes

TO ASSEMBLE

1 tablespoon (15ml) fresh lemon juice
½ teaspoon (2.5ml) fresh thyme leaves

For the Strip Steak

Preheat a water bath to 131°F (55°C).

Lightly salt and pepper the steak, then place it in a sous vide bag and seal. Place the bag in the water bath and cook for 2 to 4 hours, until heated through.

For the Roasted Brussels Sprouts

Preheat an oven to 400°F (200°C).

Cut the ends off the Brussels sprouts and discard the ends. Cut the remaining portion in half lengthwise. Toss the Brussels sprouts and garlic in olive oil, then salt and pepper them. Place them on a rimmed baking sheet, then cook, stirring once or twice, until tender, about 30 to 45 minutes.

During the last 5 or 10 minutes, add the cherry tomatoes to the baking sheet and cook until they just start to burst.

To Assemble

Take the sous vide bag out of the water and remove the cooked strip steak. Dry it off thoroughly, using paper towels or a clean dish cloth. Lightly salt the steak then quickly sear it for 1 to 2 minutes per side, just until browned, then remove from the heat.

Place the roasted Brussels sprouts and tomatoes in a bowl and drizzle with the fresh lemon juice. Add the steak, sprinkle with the thyme leaves, and serve.

> **TIP** Strip steak is sometimes cut fairly thin, so it can be hard to get a good sear on it. I recommend either using a torch or chilling it in an ice bath for 5 minutes before searing it.

PORTERHOUSE STEAK WITH FINGERLING POTATOES AND PICKLED RAMPS

COOKS: 131°F (55°C) FOR 2 TO 4 HOURS | SERVES: 4

I eat a lot of beef, but I'm still excited when a big porterhouse steak comes out on a plate. With both tenderloin and strip meat, there is a little bit for everyone on a porterhouse. I like to serve this family-style, so we can enjoy a nice presentation of the whole cut, and then carve it up for my guests.

Porterhouse steak is often enjoyed with potatoes, such as these simple pan-fried fingerlings, and some sort of pickled vegetable. This recipe includes quick pickled ramps, but they are only in season for a short time, so you can substitute green beans, sliced red onion, cauliflower florets, or even sliced fennel.

FOR THE PORTERHOUSE STEAK

1–2 pounds (450–900g) porterhouse steak

FOR THE FINGERLING POTATOES

2 pounds (900g) fingerling potatoes, cut in half lengthwise

FOR THE QUICK PICKLED RAMPS

1–2 bunches ramps, cleaned and trimmed

½ cup (118ml) apple cider vinegar

½ cup (118ml) water

2 tablespoons (30ml) sugar

¼ teaspoon (1ml) red pepper flakes

TO ASSEMBLE

Sea salt or other flaky salt

For the Porterhouse Steak

Preheat a water bath to 131°F (55°C).

Lightly salt and pepper the steak, then place it in a sous vide bag and seal. Place the bag in the water bath and cook for 2 to 4 hours, until heated through.

For the Fingerling Potatoes

Heat some oil in a pan over medium to medium-high heat. Add the potatoes and cook until tender, 10 to 20 minutes, stirring occasionally. Salt and pepper to taste, then remove from the heat.

For the Quick Pickled Ramps

Place the ramps, apple cider vinegar, water, sugar, and red pepper flakes in a pot large enough to easily hold them, and bring to a boil. Reduce the heat and let simmer for 5 minutes. Remove from the heat and let cool.

To Assemble

Take the sous vide bag out of the water and remove the cooked porterhouse steak. Dry it off thoroughly, using paper towels or a clean dish cloth. Lightly salt the steak, then quickly sear it for 1 to 2 minutes per side, just until browned. Remove it from the heat. Place the porterhouse steak on a serving platter and top with the pickled ramps. Place the fingerling potatoes around the steak. Sprinkle with the sea salt and some olive oil, then serve.

PRIME RIB WITH HORSERADISH MASHED POTATOES

COOKS: 131°F (55°C) FOR 2 TO 4 HOURS | SERVES: 4

Every year for Christmas, my family has a big discussion about what we want to eat for dinner, and we end up making prime rib. It used to be an all-day production.

Then we tried making a sous vide prime rib and we've never looked back. The convenience alone is worth it, but we have found that the meat turns out more tender, and more juicy. You lose a little in the presentation, since it's best to cut the roast into slabs under 2½" (6cm) thick, but it's a small price to pay for a stress-free holiday!

FOR THE PRIME RIB

½ teaspoon (2.5ml) garlic powder

½ teaspoon (2.5ml) onion powder

1–2 pounds (450–900g) prime rib roast

FOR THE ROASTED CARROTS

10 large carrots

2 tablespoons (30ml) olive oil

1 teaspoon (5ml) fresh thyme leaves

FOR THE HORSERADISH MASHED POTATOES

2 pounds (900g) potatoes, coarsely diced

4 tablespoons (60ml) butter, melted

⅔ cup (158ml) whole milk

½ cup (118ml) sour cream

2 tablespoons (30ml) prepared horseradish

TO ASSEMBLE

1 tablespoon (10ml) minced chives

For the Prime Rib

Preheat a water bath to 131°F (55°C).

Mix together the spices in a small bowl. Lightly salt and pepper the prime rib, then sprinkle with the spices. Place the meat in a sous vide bag, then seal. Place the bag in the water bath and cook for 2 to 4 hours, until heated through.

For the Roasted Carrots

Preheat an oven to 400°F (200°C).

Peel the carrots and cut into ¾" (19mm) chunks. Toss with the olive oil and thyme, then salt and pepper them. Place them in a roasting pan or on a rimmed baking sheet in a single layer. Roast in the oven until starting to brown and the carrots have softened and are cooked through, about 30 to 45 minutes. Once cooked, remove from the heat.

For the Horseradish Mashed Potatoes

Place the potatoes in a pot of salted water and bring to a simmer. Cook the potatoes until tender, about 10 to 20 minutes, then drain the potatoes.

Place the potatoes in a bowl with the butter, milk, sour cream, and horseradish. Mash the mixture together until it forms your preferred mashed potato texture, adding more milk or butter as needed. Season with salt and pepper.

To Assemble

Take the sous vide bag out of the water and remove the cooked prime rib roast. Dry it off thoroughly, using spaper towels or a clean dish cloth. Lightly salt the roast, then quickly sear it for 1 to 2 minutes per side, just until browned. Remove it from the heat. Slice the prime rib and serve with carrots and potatoes. Top with chives.

FLAT IRON STEAK WITH HONEY-SRIRACHA CAULIFLOWER

COOKS: 131°F (55°C) FOR 12 TO 24 HOURS | SERVES: 4

I've been eating a decent amount of cauliflower lately, and this recipe was inspired by a great Gobi Manchurian appetizer from a nearby Indian restaurant. The sweet and spicy honey-sriracha glaze seriously boosts the flavor, making it a great side dish for a steak.

Flat iron is a highly tasty cut of meat, but it can be quite tough, so sous viding it for a long time really helps it to shine. I'll usually sous vide it for 12 to 24 hours, but some people will go as long as 2 days, depending on how tender they want it.

FOR THE FLAT IRON STEAK

1–2 pounds (450–900g) flat iron steak

FOR THE HONEY-SRIRACHA CAULIFLOWER

¼ cup (60ml) honey

3 tablespoons (45ml) sriracha

2 heads cauliflower

For the Flat Iron Steak

Preheat a water bath to 131°F (55°C).

Lightly salt and pepper the steak, then place it in a sous vide bag and seal. Place the bag in the water bath and cook for 12 to 24 hours, until tenderized.

For the Honey-Sriracha Cauliflower

Preheat the oven to 400°F (200°C).

Lay aluminum foil on the bottom of a rimmed baking sheet.

Mix the honey and sriracha together in a small bowl, then season with salt and pepper.

Cut off the greens from the cauliflower and discard. Cut each head of cauliflower in half (yielding 4 pieces). Lightly brush some olive oil on the bottom of the cauliflower and place it on the sheet pan. Brush the visible sides with some of the honey-sriracha glaze. Place in the oven and cook for 30 to 60 minutes, until tender, brushing on more honey-sriracha glaze every 10 to 15 minutes.

Once tender, remove from the heat.

To Assemble

Take the sous vide bag out of the water and remove the cooked flat iron steak. Dry it off thoroughly, using paper towels or a clean dish cloth. Lightly salt the steak, then quickly sear it for 1 to 2 minutes per side, just until browned, then remove from the heat and cut into 4 serving portions.

Serve the steak and cauliflower next to each other on the plate.

HANGER STEAK FAJITAS

COOKS: 131°F (55°C) FOR 2 TO 4 HOURS | SERVES: 4

When I worked at ESPN, we used to go out to get fajitas once a week. I love the soft tortilla wrapper, sizzling meat, and crisp peppers and onions. I still get them often when I'm visiting, but for a more regular fix I have to make my own.

I usually have diced tomatoes, refried beans, Mexican rice, grated cheese, guacamole, and sour cream on the table when I'm serving these, but you can stick with any of the sides you enjoy.

FOR THE HANGER STEAK

½ teaspoon (2.5ml) ground coriander

½ teaspoon (2.5ml) ground cumin

½ teaspoon (2.5ml) garlic powder

¼ teaspoon (1ml) chipotle pepper powder

1–2 pounds (450–900g) hanger steak

FOR THE PEPPERS AND ONIONS

2 tablespoons (30ml) canola oil

2 onions, preferably Vidalia or sweet, sliced

3 bell peppers—green and red, sliced

1–2 poblano peppers, sliced

1 tablespoon (15ml) soy sauce

TO ASSEMBLE

10 tortilla wrappers

Sour cream

For the Hanger Steak

Preheat a water bath to 131°F (55°C).

Mix together the spices in a small bowl. Lightly salt and pepper the steak, then sprinkle with the spices. Place the hanger steak in a sous vide bag and seal. Place the bag in the water bath and cook for 2 to 4 hours, until heated through.

For the Peppers and Onions

Heat the canola oil in a pan over medium to medium-high heat. Add the onions and peppers, and cook until they just begin to brown and are cooked through. Add the soy sauce and toss to coat the peppers and onions. Remove from the heat and set aside.

To Assemble

Take the sous vide bag out of the water and remove the cooked hanger steak. Dry it off thoroughly, using paper towels or a clean dish cloth. Lightly salt the steak then quickly sear it for 1 to 2 minutes per side, just until browned. Remove it from the heat. Cut the hanger steak into slices.

Serve the sliced hanger steak with the tortilla wrappers, peppers and onions, and the sour cream plus additional sides to complement the fajitas.

FLANK STEAK WITH GREEN APPLE SLAW

COOKS: 131°F (55°C) FOR 2 TO 4 HOURS, OR UP TO 2 DAYS | SERVES: 4

When I was vacationing in Thailand, I ate a ton of green papaya salads. They have an amazingly tart, spicy, and umami flavor, with a crisp texture that goes great with meat. Unfortunately, it is very hard to find green papaya here in America. One of the chefs I talked to in Thailand recommended making it with Granny Smith apples. This slaw still captures the essence of the Thai dish, but is easier to replicate at home.

When sous viding flank steak, you just need to cook it long enough to heat it through, but you can cook it longer to tenderize it if you want. I prefer cooking it under 12 hours, but some people sous vide it as long as 2 days for an extra-tender steak.

FOR THE FLANK STEAK

1–2 pounds (450–900g) flank steak

FOR THE GREEN APPLE SLAW

2 Granny Smith apples

2 cloves garlic, minced

1 serrano pepper, seeded and minced

1 tablespoon (15ml) fish sauce

1 tablespoon (15ml) fresh lime juice

1 cup (237ml) shredded cabbage

½ cup (118ml) shredded carrots

8 cherry tomatoes, halved

TO ASSEMBLE

Fresh cilantro, chopped

Roasted peanuts, coarsely chopped

For the Flank Steak

Preheat a water bath to 131°F (55°C).

Lightly salt and pepper the steak then place it in a sous vide bag and seal. Place the bag in the water bath and cook for 2 to 4 hours, until heated through, or up to 2 days, until tenderized.

For the Green Apple Slaw

Wash the outside of the apples and remove the cores. Cut them into matchsticks or use a mandolin or spiralizer.

Mix together the garlic, serrano pepper, fish sauce, and lime juice. Toss the mixture with the green apples, shredded cabbage, and shredded carrots. Salt and pepper to taste, then stir in the cherry tomatoes.

To Assemble

Take the sous vide bag out of the water and remove the cooked flank steak. Dry it off thoroughly, using paper towels or a clean dish cloth. Lightly salt the steak, then quickly sear it for 1 to 2 minutes per side, just until browned Remove the steak from the heat. Slice the flank steak.

To serve, place some slices of the flank steak on a plate and top with the green apple slaw. Sprinkle the cilantro and roasted peanuts on top.

TOP ROUND WITH YAM NEUA SAUCE

COOKS: 131°F (55°C) FOR 1 TO 2 DAYS | SERVES: 4

Yam neua is a Thai beef salad with a very flavorful sauce of chili peppers, lime juice, shallots, and fish sauce. This is a more Americanized version, but it is still filled with bold Thai flavors. The sauce is tossed with beef, crisp veggies, and lots of fresh herbs.

You can use any cut of beef in this recipe, but because the sauce is so strong, I find it works well with the less flavorful cuts, like top round.

FOR THE TOP ROUND

1 teaspoon (5ml) ancho pepper powder

½ teaspoon (2.5ml) garlic powder

½ teaspoon (2.5ml) onion powder

1–2 pounds (450–900g) top round

FOR THE YAM NEUA SAUCE

2 shallots, sliced

½ Thai bird chili or serrano chili, diced

Juice of 2 limes

1 teaspoon (5ml) sugar

2 teaspoons (10ml) maple syrup

2 tablespoons (30ml) fish sauce

2 tablespoons (30ml) olive oil

TO ASSEMBLE

½ cucumber, sliced

1 large carrot, peeled, cut lengthwise, and cut into thin half moons

2 cups halved cherry tomatoes

½ cup (118ml) coarsely chopped fresh cilantro

½ cup (118ml) coarsely chopped fresh basil leaves

¼ cup (60ml) coarsely chopped fresh mint leaves

For the Top Round

Preheat a water bath to 131°F (55°C).

Mix together the spices in a small bowl. Lightly salt and pepper the top round, then sprinkle with the spices. Place the meat in a sous vide bag and seal. Place the bag in the water bath and cook for 1 to 2 days, until tenderized.

For the Yam Neua Sauce

Combine the shallots, diced chilies, lime juice, sugar, maple syrup, and fish sauce in a bowl. Salt and pepper to taste, then let sit 5 minutes. While whisking, slowly drizzle in the oil until the mixture comes together.

To Assemble

Salt the cucumber slices, then let them sit in a colander for 10 to 15 minutes to drain.

Take the sous vide bag out of the water and remove the cooked top round. Dry it off thoroughly, using paper towels or a clean dish cloth. Lightly salt the top round, then quickly sear it for 1 to 2 minutes per side, just until browned. Remove from the heat. Cut the top round into slices.

Place the top round slices, cucumber, carrots, cherry tomatoes, cilantro, basil, and mint in a bowl, then mix until thoroughly combined. Spoon out onto a plate, drizzle with the yam neua sauce, then serve.

POT ROAST WITH GARLIC MASHED POTATOES

COOKS: 176°F (80°C) FOR 12 TO 18 HOURS | SERVES: 4

I ate a lot of pot roasts growing up, usually with some vegetables and instant mashed potatoes. Now that I'm older, I still eat the occasional pot roast, but I like to make my mashed potatoes from scratch, so they have more flavor.

My preferred pot roast cut is chuck roast, which has a flaky texture when cooked to a high temperature, but you can also use short ribs, eye of round, brisket, or shank. I like 176°F (80°C) for a more traditional texture, but a pot roast cooked at 156°F (68.9°C) has an amazing texture unique to sous vide.

FOR THE POT ROAST

½ teaspoon (2.5ml) ground coriander

½ teaspoon (2.5ml) onion powder

¼ teaspoon (1ml) ground cumin

1–2 pounds (450–900g) chuck roast

FOR THE ROASTED GARLIC

8 cloves garlic

FOR THE GARLIC MASHED POTATOES

2 pounds (900g) potatoes, coarsely diced

5 tablespoons (75ml) butter, melted

⅔ cup (158ml) whole milk

FOR THE GRAVY

4 tablespoons (60ml) butter

3 tablespoons (45ml) flour

1½ cups (355ml) beef stock

½ teaspoon (2.5ml) fresh thyme leaves

For the Pot Roast

Preheat a water bath to 176°F (80°C).

Mix together the spices in a small bowl. Lightly salt and pepper the chuck roast, then sprinkle with the spices. Place the meat in a sous vide bag and seal. Place the bag in the water bath and cook for 12 to 18 hours, until tenderized.

For the Roasted Garlic

Peel the garlic cloves and drizzle with some olive oil and salt; wrap in tinfoil, then place in a 400°F (200°C) oven until soft, about 30 to 45 minutes. Remove and set aside to cool slightly.

For the Garlic Mashed Potatoes

Place the potatoes in a pot of salted water and bring to a simmer. Cook the potatoes until tender, about 10 to 20 minutes, then drain them.

Place the potatoes in a bowl with the butter, milk, and roasted garlic. Mash the mixture together until it reaches your preferred mashed potato texture, adding more milk or butter as needed. Season with salt and pepper.

> TIP I prefer rustic mashed potatoes, but for a more refined presentation and a smoother consistency you can peel the potatoes and, once cooked, whip them with a wooden spoon or use a potato ricer.

For the gravy

Melt the butter in pan over medium heat. Once the butter stops frothing, add the flour and mix until it forms a paste. Incorporate the beef stock and thyme by whisking to combine with the flour paste. Bring to a boil and then remove from the heat. Salt and pepper to taste.

To Assemble

Take the sous vide bag out of the water and carefully remove the chuck roast so as not to break it apart. Reserve the juices from the bag and whisk them into the gravy. Dry it off thoroughly, using paper towels or a clean dish cloth. Lightly salt the roast, then quickly sear it in a pan for 1 to 2 minutes per side, just until browned, then remove from the heat.

Place a spoonful or two of the mashed potatoes on a plate and top with some of the chuck roast. Spoon some of the gravy on top, then serve.

CHUCK ROAST WITH HERBED BUTTER AND SAUTÉED ONIONS

COOKS: 131°F (55°C) FOR 36 TO 60 HOURS | SERVES: 4

Chuck roast is a magical cut when cooked for a long period. It turns into something resembling the texture and flavor of a rib eye, at a fraction of the cost. I usually cook mine around 36 hours so it maintains some bite, but many people enjoy theirs cooked up to 60 hours for a super-tender steak.

This recipe highlights the transformation of the chuck roast by slicing it into strips and serving it simply with a flavorful herb butter and sautéed onions.

FOR THE CHUCK ROAST

1 teaspoon (5ml) garlic powder

½ teaspoon (2.5ml) paprika

1–2 pounds (450–900g) chuck roast

FOR THE HERB BUTTER

4 tablespoons (60ml) unsalted butter

2 tablespoons (30ml) finely chopped fresh parsley

Juice of ¼ lemon

Coarse salt

Freshly cracked black pepper

FOR THE SAUTEED ONIONS

3 onions, preferably Vidalia or sweet, sliced

4 cloves garlic, minced

TO ASSEMBLE

2 tablespoons (30ml) chopped fresh basil leaves

Sea salt (flaky or coarsely ground)

For the Chuck Roast

Preheat a water bath to 131°F (55°C).

Mix together the spices in a small bowl. Lightly salt and pepper the chuck roast, then sprinkle with the spices. Place the meat in a sous vide bag and seal. Place the bag in the water bath and cook for 36 to 60 hours, until tenderized.

For the Herb Butter

Let the butter soften at room temperature.

Place the butter, parsley, and lemon juice in a bowl, then lightly salt and pepper. Mash the ingredients together until well combined.

For the Sautéed Onions

Heat some oil in a pan over medium to medium-high heat. Add the onions and garlic, stirring until they just begin to brown and are cooked through, about 10 to 25 minutes. Remove from the heat and set aside.

To Assemble

Take the sous vide bag out of the water and remove the cooked chuck roast. Dry it off thoroughly, using paper towels or a clean dish cloth. Lightly salt the roast then quickly sear it for 1 to 2 minutes per side, just until browned. Remove it from the heat. Slice the roast.

To serve, place the meat on a plate and add a few pats of herb butter. Top with the sautéed onions and basil leaves, and sprinkle with the sea salt.

BACON-CHEDDAR CHEESEBURGERS

COOKS: 138°F (58.9°C) FOR 2 TO 4 HOURS | SERVES: 4

Bacon cheeseburgers are among my favorite meals, and I love to try all different styles and preparations. At home, you can cook burgers to any temperature as long as you follow good safety guidelines and use trusted meat, or grind your own, but that can be a huge hassle. Using sous vide allows you to cook your burgers to any temperature you like and hold it there long enough to fully pasteurize them. This means you can safely eat grocery store ground beef medium-rare without any concerns.

I prefer my burgers around 138°F (58.9°C), but you can safely go as low as 130°F (54.4°C) and still pasteurize it.

FOR THE CHEESEBURGERS

4 hamburger patties, about 5 ounces (113g) each, preferably at least 1" (25mm) thick

TO ASSEMBLE

4 hamburger buns

4 slices cheddar cheese

4 slices cooked bacon

4 tomato slices

4 large lettuce leaves

4 whole dill pickles

Potato chips

For the Cheeseburgers

Preheat a water bath to 138°F (58.9°C).

Lightly salt and pepper the patties, then place in a sous vide bag and lightly seal. Place the bag in the water bath and cook for 2 to 4 hours, until pasteurized.

To Assemble

Take the sous vide bag out of the water and remove the cooked patties. Dry them off thoroughly, using paper towels or a clean dish cloth. Lightly salt the hamburger patties, then quickly sear them for 1 to 2 minutes per side, just until browned. Remove from the heat.

Place a hamburger patty on a bun, then top with the cheddar cheese, bacon, tomato, and lettuce. Serve with a dill pickle and the potato chips.

> **TIP** When sealing hamburgers or other ground meats, use the lightest setting on the vacuum sealer, or a Ziploc bag, so you don't crush the patties and flatten them out too much.

BRAISED SHORT RIBS WITH A RED WINE REDUCTION AND MASHED SWEET POTATOES

COOKS: 156°F (68.9°C) FOR 1 TO 2 DAYS | SERVES: 4

I didn't eat short ribs much until I got into sous vide, but now I really enjoy them. They are a rich, fatty cut that is traditionally braised, or in Korean barbecue, sliced really thin and grilled. With sous vide you have a few options, ranging from a steaklike cook, sous vided at 131°F (55°C), up to a more traditional cook, sous vided at 176°F (80°C). For this recipe I'll stick to 156°F (68.9°C), which results in a tender, barely braised short rib that still retains some of its structure.

I pair it with a flavorful red wine reduction and some mashed sweet potatoes to cut the richness of the short ribs.

FOR THE BRAISED SHORT RIBS

1–2 pounds (450–900g) beef short ribs

FOR THE RED WINE REDUCTION

2 teaspoons (10ml) olive oil

1 shallot, minced

2 cloves garlic, minced

2 cups (473ml) red wine

2 teaspoons (10ml) chopped fresh rosemary leaves

¼ teaspoon (1ml) ground cloves

2–3 teaspoons (10–15ml) sugar

FOR THE MASHED SWEET POTATOES

2 pounds (900g) sweet potatoes, peeled and coarsely diced

5 tablespoons (75ml) butter, melted

⅔ cup (158ml) whole milk

1 tablespoon (15ml) molasses

For the Braised Short Ribs

Preheat a water bath to 156°F (68.9°C).

Lightly salt and pepper the short ribs, then place them in a sous vide bag and seal. Place the bag in the water bath and cook for 1 to 2 days, until tenderized.

For the Red Wine Reduction

Combine the oil, shallots, and garlic in a pan, and place over medium heat. Cook until the shallots are softened, about 3 to 5 minutes. Add the wine, rosemary, and ground cloves, then bring to a boil. Reduce the heat, add the sugar, and let simmer until the sauce has reduced by about 30 percent, about 25 to 40 minutes.

For the Mashed Sweet Potatoes

Place the sweet potatoes in a pot of salted water and bring to a simmer. Cook the sweet potatoes until tender, about 10 to 20 minutes, then drain the sweet potatoes.

Place the sweet potatoes in a bowl with the butter, milk, and molasses. Mash the mixture together until it reaches your preferred mashed sweet potato consistency, adding more milk or butter as needed. Season with salt and pepper.

2 tablespoons (30ml) chopped
fresh basil leaves

Zest of 1 orange

To Assemble

Take the sous vide bag out of the water and remove the cooked short ribs. Dry them off thoroughly, using paper towels or a clean dish cloth. Lightly salt the short ribs then quickly sear them for 1 to 2 minutes per side, just until browned. Remove them from the heat.

To serve, place a spoonful of the mashed sweet potatoes on a plate and top with a short rib or two. Sprinkle with the basil leaves and orange zest. Drizzle with the red wine reduction.

> TIP I often use a cabernet sauvignon for this recipe, but you can use pinot noir, zinfandel, or any other full and fruity wine. It also doesn't have to be a great bottle of wine: Anything decent that you'd feel comfortable drinking casually will do.

TERIYAKI-GLAZED SHORT RIBS WITH ROASTED CAULIFLOWER PUREE

COOKS: 131°F (55°C) FOR 2 TO 3 DAYS | SERVES: 4

I can eat a great teriyaki sauce on just about anything, but it pairs exceptionally well with rich and fatty short ribs. Once the ribs are finished sous viding, they are quickly glazed with the teriyaki sauce on a grill, under a broiler, or with a torch. This creates a sweet and sticky coating that elevates the flavor of the ribs.

These short ribs are cooked at 131°F (55°C), which results in a steaklike consistency, not the braiselike texture you are used to with traditional short ribs. I like to serve them with a roasted cauliflower puree to cut the richness of the dish. This sauce also pairs beautifully with pork chops, duck breast, and chicken breasts.

FOR THE SHORT RIBS

1–2 pounds (450–900g) beef short ribs

FOR THE TERIYAKI GLAZE

⅓ cup (78ml) soy sauce

¼ cup (60ml) hoisin sauce

¼ cup (60ml) brown sugar

½ cup (118ml) diced pineapple

⅓ fresh red chili or jalapeño pepper, diced

2 cloves garlic, diced

1 tablespoon (15ml) freshly grated ginger

3 tablespoons (45ml) rice vinegar

FOR THE ROASTED CAULIFLOWER PUREE

1 head of cauliflower, coarsely chopped

5 cloves garlic, coarsely chopped

1 shallot, minced

½ teaspoon (2.5ml) fresh thyme leaves

½ cup (118ml) chicken stock

1 tablespoon (15ml) fresh lemon juice

1 tablespoon (15ml) butter

For the Short Ribs

Preheat a water bath to 131°F (55°C).

Lightly salt and pepper the ribs, then place them in a sous vide bag and seal. Place the bag in the water bath and cook for 2 to 3 days, until tenderized.

For the Teriyaki Glaze

In a medium saucepan, combine all the teriyaki glaze ingredients and bring to a simmer. Gently simmer for 5 to 10 minutes, then remove from the heat and puree, using a blender or a food processor.

For the Roasted Cauliflower Puree

Preheat an oven to 400°F (200°C).

Toss the cauliflower, garlic, shallots, and thyme in enough olive oil to lightly coat, then salt and pepper to taste. Place on a rimmed baking sheet, then cook, stirring once or twice, about 20 to 30 minutes or until tender.

Place the roasted vegetables, chicken stock, lemon juice, and butter in a food processor and process until smooth.

1 red chili, thinly sliced

3 tablespoons (45ml) coarsely chopped roasted peanuts

2 tablespoons (30ml) chopped fresh basil leaves

To Assemble

Take the sous vide bag out of the water and remove the cooked short ribs. Dry them off thoroughly, using paper towels or a clean dish cloth. Lightly salt the short ribs, then brush them with the teriyaki glaze. Quickly sear the short ribs for 1 minute per side, then add more glaze and sear for another minute. Repeat a few times until the glaze has coated the short ribs. Remove the ribs from the heat.

Place a spoonful of the cauliflower puree on a plate and top with a short rib or two. Drizzle some more of the teriyaki glaze on top. Add a few slices of red chili and the peanuts. Sprinkle some basil leaves on top, then serve.

> TIP If you prefer more of a sauce than a glaze, you can add 6 ounces (170g) of pineapple juice to the teriyaki glaze and reduce the amount of soy sauce by half.

SMOKED BBQ BRISKET WITH GRILLED SUMMER SQUASH AND ONIONS

COOKS: 156°F (68.9°C) FOR 1 TO 2 DAYS | SERVES: 4

It's hard to truly replicate a traditionally smoked brisket using sous vide, but this method does allow you to make an exceptionally tender and juicy brisket that, when finished on a smoker, maintains a lot of that wonderful smoky flavor. You can use a dedicated smoker or a grill with wood chips. And if you don't have access to a smoker, you can always add a teaspoon or two (5–10ml) of liquid smoke to the bag during the sous vide process and finish it with a sear, as in the other recipes in this chapter.

When I am cooking a BBQ brisket that I will smoke, I prefer to use 156°F (68.9°C) because it turns out very tender and moist, but doesn't fall apart. If you want a more shreddable texture, you can go all the way up to 176°F (80°C) with a shorter time.

In this recipe I pair the brisket with some grilled vegetables, but you can serve it with any traditional BBQ sides or sauces that appeal to you.

FOR THE BRISKET

1 teaspoon (5ml) ancho pepper powder

1 teaspoon (5ml) smoked paprika

1 teaspoon (5ml) dried thyme

½ teaspoon (2.5ml) mustard powder

½ teaspoon (2.5ml) ground coriander

2–3 pounds (900–1,350g) brisket

FOR THE SUMMER SQUASH AND ONIONS

3 zucchini

3 yellow crookneck summer squash

2 onions

For the Brisket

Preheat a water bath to 156°F (68.9°C).

Mix together the spices in a bowl. Lightly salt and pepper the brisket, then sprinkle with the spices. Place the brisket in a sous vide bag and seal. Place the bag in the water bath and cook for 1 to 2 days, until tenderized. Remove from the sous vide bath and chill in an ice bath for at least 30 to 60 minutes.

For the Summer Squash and Onions

Preheat a grill to high heat.

Wash the zucchini and crookneck squash and then cut them lengthwise into ½" (13mm) slabs. Peel the onions and then cut them into ½" (13mm) slabs, trying to keep the rings whole. Salt and pepper the squash and onions, then drizzle with oil.

Place the vegetables on the grill and cook until tender, turning a few times to ensure even cooking. Remove from the heat.

To Assemble

Prepare a smoker to 200°F to 250°F (93.3°C–121.1°C)

Remove the chilled brisket from the sous vide bag and dry thoroughly, using paper towels or a clean dish cloth. Lightly salt the brisket, place it in the smoker. Smoke the brisket until the middle reaches 140°F to 150°F (60°C–65.6°C) then remove from the heat. Cut the brisket into slices and serve with the summer squash and onions.

> **TIP** I love the flavor of grilled onions, but they can be hard to keep together when you're turning them on the grill. If you run into trouble, I recommend using toothpicks or skewers to keep the onion rings in place.

LAMB CHOPS WITH CHARMOULA

COOKS: 130°F (54.4°C) FOR 2 TO 4 HOURS | SERVES: 4

I was first introduced to charmoula last year and I've fallen in love with it. It's a spicy and herb-filled condiment with origins in Morocco and Libya. With minor tweaks to the herbs used, I've paired it with anything from fish to turkey to beef, and here I serve a mint-heavy version with lamb chops. The charmoula can be made as spicy, or as mild, as you like by varying the amount of serrano pepper you use in it.

I often serve these lamb chops with a roasted vegetable medley or a light side salad.

FOR THE LAMB CHOPS

1–2 pounds (450–900g) lamb chops

FOR THE CHARMOULA

1 clove garlic, minced

½ cup (118ml) chopped fresh parsley

¼ cup (60ml) chopped fresh cilantro

2 tablespoons (30ml) chopped fresh mint leaves

¼ cup (60ml) olive oil

Zest of 1 lemon

Juice of ½ lemon, about 1 tablespoon (15ml)

1 serrano pepper, finely chopped

½ teaspoon (2.5ml) ground cumin

½ teaspoon (2.5ml) ground coriander

TO ASSEMBLE

2 tablespoons (30ml) chopped fresh Italian parsley

1 tablespoon (15ml) chopped fresh mint

For the Lamb Chops

Preheat a water bath to 130°F (54.4°C).

Lightly salt and pepper the lamb chops, then place them in a sous vide bag and seal. Place the bag in the water bath and cook for 2 to 4 hours, until heated through.

For the Charmoula

Place all of the ingredients in a bowl and mix together.

To Assemble

Take the sous vide bag out of the water and remove the cooked lamb chops. Dry them off thoroughly, using paper towels or a clean dish cloth. Lightly salt the lamb chops, then quickly sear them for 1 to 2 minutes per side, just until browned. Remove from the heat.

To serve, place one or two lamb chops on a plate. Spoon some of the charmoula on top. Sprinkle with the chopped parsley and mint.

RACK OF LAMB WITH CHERRY CHUTNEY GLAZE

COOKS: 130°F (54.4°C) FOR 2 TO 4 HOURS | SERVES: 4

I find this cherry chutney glaze an easy way to add a lot of flavor to a rack of lamb. It is heavily spiced, with ginger, allspice, and cinnamon, and gains loads of sweetness from the cherries, brown sugar, and fruit juices.

I prefer to cook the rack of lamb whole, glaze it, and then cut it into serving portions. This helps prevent it from overcooking while the glaze sets. Depending on whether I'm serving this lamb for lunch or dinner, I like to pair it with mashed potatoes, sautéed green beans, or even potatoes au gratin.

FOR THE RACK OF LAMB

1–2 racks of lamb (about 1¼–2 lbs per rack)

FOR THE CHERRY CHUTNEY GLAZE

¼ onion, diced

1 cup (237ml) coarsely diced, pitted cherries (about 15)

2 teaspoons (10ml) minced fresh ginger

1 tablespoon (15ml) balsamic vinegar

2 tablespoons (30ml) spiced rum

⅛ teaspoon (0.5ml) chili powder, preferably chipotle

¼ teaspoon (1ml) allspice

¼ teaspoon (1ml) cinnamon

¼ cup (60ml) fresh orange juice

¼ cup (60ml) pomegranate juice

¼ cup (60ml) brown sugar

TO ASSEMBLE

1 tablespoon (15ml) minced fresh rosemary

For the Racks of Lamb

Preheat a water bath to 130°F (54.4°C).

Lightly salt and pepper the racks of lamb, then place them in a sous vide bag and seal. Place the bag in the water bath and cook for 2 to 4 hours, until heated through.

For the Cherry Chutney Glaze

Heat some olive oil in a pan over medium heat. Add the onions and cook until they just start to brown, about 5–8 minutes Add the cherries and ginger, and cook for 5 minutes. Add the remaining ingredients and cook for 5 minutes, then puree lightly in a blender or food processor, adding more orange juice as needed until it is thinned enough to brush onto the meat.

To Assemble

Take the sous vide bag out of the water and remove the cooked racks of lamb. Dry them off thoroughly, using paper towels or a clean dish cloth. Lightly salt the racks of lamb, then brush them with the cherry chutney glaze. Quickly sear the racks of lamb for 1 minute per side, then add more glaze and sear for another minute. Repeat a few times until the glaze has coated the racks of lamb. Remove the ribs from the heat and cut into serving portions, usually one or two ribs.

Serve the lamb portions with extra cherry chutney glaze and fresh rosemary sprinkled on top.

LAMB SHOULDER WITH GRILLED VEGETABLES

COOKS: 165°F (73.9°C) FOR 18 TO 24 HOURS | SERVES: 4

Rich and meaty lamb shoulder pairs well with a garlic, parsley, and mint-based sauce. It keeps the dish light and highlights the taste of the lamb. Adding grilled vegetables introduces more flavor and texture to the dish, while the farro helps to bulk it up into a complete meal.

This recipe calls for the lamb shoulder to be cooked at 165°F (73.9°C), which will result in a traditional braiselike texture. If you want a more lamb chop–like texture, you can reduce the temperature to 131°F (55°C) and increase the time to 1 to 2 days.

FOR THE LAMB SHOULDER

1 teaspoon (5ml) garlic powder

½ teaspoon (2.5ml) paprika

1–2 pounds (450–900g) lamb shoulder

2 sprigs fresh rosemary

2 sprigs fresh thyme

FOR THE GARLIC-PARSLEY SAUCE

2 cups (473ml) lightly packed chopped fresh parsley

10–15 fresh mint leaves

2 cloves garlic, coarsely chopped

½ cup (118ml) olive oil

½ cup (118ml) water

¼ cup (60ml) freshly grated parmesan cheese

2 tablespoons (30ml) fresh lemon juice

FOR THE GRILLED VEGETABLES

2 zucchini

1 eggplant

2 red bell peppers

2 orange bell peppers

TO ASSEMBLE

2 cups (473ml) cooked farro

2 tablespoons (30ml) chopped fresh parsley

For the Lamb Shoulder

Preheat a water bath to 165°F (73.9°C).

Mix together the dried spices in a bowl. Lightly salt and pepper the lamb shoulder, then sprinkle with the spice mix. Place the lamb shoulder in a sous vide bag with the rosemary and thyme, then seal the bag. Cook for 18 to 24 hours, until tenderized.

For the Garlic-Parsley Sauce

Place all the ingredients in a blender or food processor and process until smooth. Salt and pepper to taste.

For the Grilled Vegetables

Remove the stem from each zucchini and cut each one in half lengthwise. Remove the stem from the eggplant and cut lengthwise into slabs. Remove the stem and seeds of the peppers, then cut into whole sides. Toss the vegetables with olive oil, then salt and pepper them.

Cook all the vegetables on the grill, or under a broiler, until they have taken on color and become tender. Remove from the heat and cut into strips.

To Assemble

Take the sous vide bag out of the water and remove the cooked lamb shoulder. Dry it off thoroughly, using paper towels or a clean dish cloth. Lightly salt the lamb shoulder, then quickly sear it for 1 to 2 minutes per side, just until browned. Remove it from the heat and cut into 4 serving portions.

To serve, place a spoonful of farro on a plate next to the grilled vegetables. Top with a portion of lamb shoulder, then drizzle with the garlic-parsley sauce. Sprinkle with the fresh parsley.

ROSEMARY LEG OF LAMB WITH ROASTED ROOT VEGETABLES

COOKS: 130°F (54.4°C) FOR 2 TO 4 HOURS, OR UP TO 24 HOURS | SERVES: 4

Leg of lamb is a classic family dinner dish. Using sous vide to cook it ensures that it never gets dried out and is perfectly cooked, through and through. Adding some rosemary in the sous vide pouch infuses the meat with the aroma and flavor of rosemary without overpowering it.

I usually cook my leg of lamb until just heated through, but the tenderness of leg of lamb can vary considerably, and it can be cooked up to 24 hours if you want to tenderize it more.

FOR THE LEG OF LAMB

1–2 pounds (450–900g) leg of lamb

½ teaspoon (2.5ml) garlic powder

2 fresh rosemary sprigs

FOR THE ROASTED VEGETABLES

6 large carrots, peeled and coarsely chopped

1 pound (450g) fingerling potatoes, coarsely chopped

1 sweet onion, diced

2 parsnips, peeled and diced

1 tablespoon (15ml) minced fresh rosemary leaves

6 cloves garlic, coarsely chopped

TO ASSEMBLE

1 orange

For the Leg of Lamb

Preheat a water bath to 130°F (54.4°C).

Lightly salt and pepper the lamb, then sprinkle with the garlic powder. Place the leg of lamb in a sous vide bag, position the rosemary sprigs on top, then seal. Place the bag in the water bath and cook for 2 to 4 hours, until heated through, or up to 24 hours until tenderized.

For the Roasted Vegetables

Preheat an oven to 400°F (200°C).

Toss all the ingredients together with olive oil, then salt and pepper them. Place on a rimmed baking sheet, then cook, stirring once or twice, about 30 to 60 minutes, or until tender.

To Assemble

Take the sous vide bag out of the water bath and remove the cooked leg of lamb. Dry it off thoroughly, using paper towels or a clean dish cloth. Lightly salt the lamb, then quickly sear it for 1 to 2 minutes per side, just until browned. Remove from the heat. Cut the lamb into serving portions.

Place the roasted root vegetables on a plate and top with a portion of lamb. Zest the orange on top, then serve.

CHAPTER 2

Pork

PORK SOUS VIDE

Pork really shines when sous vided. It turns out super-moist and much more tender than it does with any other cooking technique. It's also safer to eat because you can fully pasteurize it without overcooking it. The recommendations below work for pork as well as boar, though if you are eating wild game you should become aware of the pathogens they may harbor, and what temperatures are needed to kill them, as it may differ from beef and pork.

TENDER AND CHOPLIKE PORK

In my view, the optimal temperature for sous vide pork is 140°F (60°C), though I sometimes cook it lower when I want to put a solid sear on it. Most people were raised on pork cooked above 155°F (68.3°C) or even 165°F (73.9°C) and can't stand having any pink on the inside, so 145°F (62.8°C) might work best for them. That's also the temperature I often cook at when I have guests who might be squeamish. However, from a safety perspective, as long as you cook it long enough to pasteurize it, 135°F (57.2°C) is just as safe as 165°F (73.9°C).

BRAISELIKE PORK

Many cuts work exceptionally well when cooked at higher temperatures to develop a "braise-like" texture, the most famous of which is probably pulled pork. Most braiselike temperatures are above 150°F (65.6°C). The temperatures I recommend starting with are:

156°F (68.9°C) for a shreddable, but still firm texture
165°F (73.9°C) for a more fall-apart texture
176°F (80°C) for a really fall-apart texture

PORK TIMING

Tender cuts only require you to cook them long enough to heat them through or pasteurize them, if desired. This will usually be between 2 and 4 hours. For tough cuts, it can take up to several days to fully tenderize them. Check the cooking times for specific cuts of pork in the charts in the back of the book.

PORK CHOPS WITH VEGETABLE STIR FRY

COOKS: 140°F (60°C) FOR 2 TO 4 HOURS | SERVES: 4

Pork chops are one of my favorite types of meat to cook sous vide, the difference between them and most traditionally cooked pork chops is huge. With the lower temperature used in sous viding, the pork retains more moisture and doesn't become tough, which really helps it shine.

I often pair pork chops with this simple vegetable stir-fry. It's quick to put together, but still has a lot of flavor. It's also exceptionally versatile, and it's a great meal to have planned when you go by the local farmers' market, because you can easily incorporate whatever vegetables are in season.

FOR THE PORK CHOPS

½ teaspoon (2.5ml) garlic powder

¼ teaspoon (1ml) ground cumin

1–2 pounds (450–900g) pork chops

FOR THE VEGETABLE STIR-FRY

1 red onion, diced

½ pound (225g) shitake mushrooms

1 red bell pepper, diced

3 cloves garlic, minced

1 tablespoon (15ml) minced ginger

1 cup (237ml) broccoli florets

1 tablespoon (15ml) water

1 tablespoon (15ml) soy sauce

1 tablespoon (15ml) fresh lemon juice

1 teaspoon (5ml) fish sauce

1 teaspoon (5ml) honey

TO ASSEMBLE

2 tablespoons (30ml) chopped fresh basil leaves

For the Pork Chops

Preheat a water bath to 140°F (60°C).

Mix together the spices in a small bowl. Lightly salt and pepper the pork chops, then sprinkle with the spices. Place the pork in a sous vide bag and seal. Place the bag in the water bath and cook for 2 to 4 hours until heated through or pasteurized.

For the Vegetable Stir-Fry

Heat some oil in a pan over medium-high heat. Add the onion and cook until beginning to soften. Add the shitake mushrooms, red pepper, garlic, and ginger, then cook until the mixture starts to soften. Add the broccoli, water, soy sauce, lemon juice, and fish sauce, then cover and cook until tender. Drizzle in the honey and stir to combine. Remove from the heat then salt and pepper to taste.

To Assemble

Take the sous vide bag out of the water and remove the cooked pork. Dry it off thoroughly, using paper towels or a clean dish cloth. Lightly salt the pork chops, then quickly sear them for 1 to 2 minutes per side, just until browned. Remove from the heat and cut into 4 portions.

To serve, spoon the vegetable stir-fry onto a plate and top with a pork chop portion. Sprinkle with the basil leaves and drizzle with olive oil.

PORK CHOPS WITH SUMMER SALSA

COOKS: 140°F (60°C) FOR 2 TO 4 HOURS | SERVES: 4

This summer salsa is the perfect side when I am looking for a light dinner that still packs a big flavor punch. It combines sweet cherry tomatoes and corn with multiple herbs, sharp red onion, and crunchy zucchini, and is finished with some red wine vinegar and olive oil to round it out. It complements pork chops, especially fattier ones from a good farm, though I've also used it on steak and chicken with great success.

FOR THE PORK CHOPS

½ teaspoon (2.5ml) garlic powder

¼ teaspoon (1ml) ground cumin

1–2 pounds (450–900g) pork chops

FOR THE SUMMER SALSA

1 cup (237ml) halved cherry tomatoes

1 cup (237ml) diced zucchini

1 cup (237ml) cooked corn kernels

¼ red onion, diced

2 tablespoons (30ml) coarsely chopped fresh basil leaves

2 tablespoons (30ml) coarsely chopped fresh oregano leaves

1 tablespoon (15ml) red wine vinegar

1 tablespoon (15ml) olive oil

TO ASSEMBLE

2 tablespoons (30ml) chopped fresh basil leaves

For the Pork Chops

Preheat a water bath to 140°F (60°C).

Mix together the spices in a small bowl. Lightly salt and pepper the pork chops, then sprinkle them with the spices. Place the pork in a sous vide bag and seal. Place the bag in the water bath and cook for 2 to 4 hours until heated through or pasteurized.

For the Summer Salsa

To make the salsa mix all the ingredients in a bowl.

Salt and pepper to taste.

To Assemble

Take the sous vide bag out of the water and remove the cooked pork. Dry it off thoroughly, using paper towels or a clean dish cloth. Lightly salt the pork chops, then quickly sear them for 1 to 2 minutes per side, just until browned. Remove them from the heat and cut into 4 portions.

To serve, place a pork chop portion on a plate and top with the summer salsa. Sprinkle with the basil leaves and drizzle with olive oil.

PORK LOIN ROAST WITH CORN, BEAN, AND KALE SALAD

COOKS: 140°F (60°C) FOR 2 TO 4 HOURS | SERVES: 4

Pork loin tends to become dry and tough when it is cooked traditionally. When sous vided, it retains its moisture and is tender all the way through. When I'm just looking for an easy weeknight meal, I'll pair the pork loin with this corn, bean, and kale salad. It's flavorful and nutritious, and always leaves me feeling full without being stuffed.

FOR THE PORK LOIN

1–2 pounds (450–900g) pork loin

FOR THE CORN, BEAN, AND KALE SALAD

2 shallots, sliced

1 bunch kale, washed and chopped

7 cloves garlic, minced

2 tablespoons (30ml) sherry vinegar

1 cup (237ml) cooked corn kernels

1 cup (237ml) cooked pinto beans

TO ASSEMBLE

Fresh parsley

For the Pork Loin

Preheat a water bath to 140°F (60°C).

Lightly salt and pepper the pork, then seal in a sous vide bag. Place the bag in the water bath and cook for 2 to 4 hours until heated through or pasteurized.

For the Corn, Bean, and Kale Salad

Heat some oil in a pan over medium heat. Add the shallots and cook until tender. Add the kale, garlic, and vinegar, then cover and let the mixture cook until the kale is tender, about 10 to 20 minutes, stirring occasionally and adding small amounts of water as needed. Stir in the corn and beans, then season with salt and pepper.

To Assemble

Take the sous vide bag out of the water and remove the cooked pork. Dry it off thoroughly, using paper towels or a clean dish cloth. Lightly salt the pork loin, then quickly sear it for 1 to 2 minutes per side, just until browned. Remove the pork loin from the heat and cut it into thick slices.

To serve, place a spoonful of the salad on a plate and top with several slices of the pork loin. Sprinkle with some fresh parsley and drizzle with olive oil.

JERKED PORK LOIN WITH PLANTAINS AND BLACK BEANS

COOKS: 140°F (60°C) FOR 2 TO 4 HOURS | SERVES: 4

Growing up in Utah, I was unfamiliar with jerked foods, but I fell in love with them after I got married. My wife has a close family friend from Jamaica and every other year we would go there with her for Thanksgiving. During the trip we would repeatedly get jerked chicken from the roadside stands and it was always amazing.

This is my own take on trying to replicate the flavors at home. There are a lot of ingredients, but this recipe makes plenty of spice mixture, so put the leftovers in a sealed container in your cabinet and it will last for weeks. Making it yourself also allows you to vary the level of spice to suit your own palate. And while I'm sure those roadside cooks wouldn't be impressed, I've gotten nothing but rave reviews from everyone who has tried it!

FOR THE JERKED PORK LOIN

⅓ cup (78ml) dark brown sugar

¼ cup (60ml) salt, plus more for seasoning

1 tablespoon (15ml) black pepper

1 tablespoon (15ml) garlic powder

1 tablespoon (15ml) onion powder

1–3 teaspoons (5–15ml) scotch bonnet or habanero chili powder

2 teaspoons (10ml) dried thyme

1 teaspoon (5ml) ground coriander

1 teaspoon (5ml) allspice

1 teaspoon (5ml) ground cumin

½ teaspoon (2.5ml) dried ginger

½ teaspoon (2.5ml) ground cinnamon

¼ teaspoon (1ml) ground cloves

¼ teaspoon (1ml) ground nutmeg

1–2 pounds (450–900g) pork loin

FOR THE FRIED PLANTAINS

2 plantains, peeled and thickly sliced

For the Jerked Pork Loin

Preheat a water bath to 140°F (60°C).

Mix all the spices together in a bowl. Lightly salt and pepper the pork, then sprinkle with the spice mixture. Place the pork loin in a sous vide bag and seal. Place the bag in the water bath and cook for 2 to 4 hours until heated through or pasteurized.

For the Fried Plantains

Heat some oil in a pan over medium-high heat. Add the plantains in a single layer and cook until they start to brown. Flip them and repeat until tender.

> TIP If you can't find scotch bonnet or habanero chili powder, you can substitute other spicy chili powders, like cayenne or chipotle. It will change the flavor profile, but it should still turn out just fine.

2 cups (473ml) cooked black beans

1 mango, peeled and diced

Fresh oregano leaves, chopped

4 lime wedges

To Assemble

Take the sous vide bag out of the water and remove the cooked pork. Dry it off thoroughly, using paper towels or a clean dish cloth. Lightly salt the pork loin, then quickly sear it for 1 to 2 minutes per side, just until browned. Remove the pork loin from the heat and cut it into thick slices.

To serve, place a spoonful of black beans on a plate and top with several slices of pork loin. Top with the mango, chopped oregano, and a lime wedge.

PORK TENDERLOIN WITH PEA PESTO

COOKS: 140°F (60°C) FOR 2 TO 4 HOURS | SERVES: 4

I first discovered this pea pesto about five years ago. It's a bright, tasty topping that I have used for everything from a sauce for meat to a dip for vegetables. It is terrific in spring or summer, when you are trying to lighten up a dish while still boosting flavor. It goes especially well with the super-tender sous vide pork tenderloin, since it adds texture and background notes to that sometimes blander cut.

FOR THE PORK TENDERLOIN

½ tablespoon garlic powder

¼ tablespoon coriander

¼ tablespoon cumin

¼ tablespoon paprika

1–2 pounds (450–900g) pork tenderloin

FOR THE PEA PESTO

2 cloves garlic, roughly chopped

1 tablespoon (15ml) fresh lemon juice

2 tablespoons (30ml) freshly grated parmesan cheese

2 tablespoons (30ml) olive oil

2 teaspoons (10ml) chopped fresh basil leaves

1 teaspoon (5ml) chopped fresh tarragon leaves

3 fresh mint leaves, chopped

1 cup (237ml) frozen peas, thawed

TO ASSEMBLE

2 tablespoons (30ml) pine nuts

For the Pork Tenderloin

Preheat a water bath to 140°F (60°C).

Mix the spices together in a small bowl. Salt and pepper the tenderloin, then sprinkle with the spice mixture. Place the pork in a sous vide bag and seal. Place the bag in the water bath and cook for 2 to 4 hours until heated through or pasteurized

For the Pea Pesto

Place all the ingredients in a blender or food processor and process until it forms a smooth puree. Salt and pepper to taste, adding water as needed to thin it out until it is the consistency you desire. It is ready to serve at this point, but can benefit from resting in the refrigerator for a few hours for the flavors to fully meld.

To Assemble

Take the sous vide bag out of the water and remove the cooked pork. Dry it off thoroughly, using paper towels or a clean dish cloth. Lightly salt the pork tenderloin, then quickly sear it for 1 to 2 minutes per side, just until browned. Remove it from the heat and cut it into slices.

To serve, place several slices of the pork tenderloin on a plate and top with a few spoonfuls of the pea pesto. Drizzle with olive oil and sprinkle with pine nuts.

ITALIAN SAUSAGE GRINDERS

COOKS: 140°F (60°C) FOR 2 TO 4 HOURS | SERVES: 4

I always struggled when cooking sausages, trying to balance searing the outside and making sure the middle of the sausage was fully cooked. Whenever I'd overcook them, the sausage turned out so dry. Now that I sous vide sausage, it's always perfect, juicy, and super-flavorful . . . without any of the stress!

You can serve sausage in a variety of ways, but one of my favorites is as the filling in a grinder. Once the sausage is seared, you place it on a toasted hoagie roll, top it with peppers, onions, and marinara sauce, then melt a lot of gooey mozzarella cheese on top of it. It's a hearty, flavorful meal that everyone loves.

FOR THE PORK SAUSAGE

1 pound (450g) sweet Italian sausage links

FOR THE PEPPERS AND ONIONS

1 onion, sliced into ¼" (6mm) strips

4 cloves garlic, minced

1 red bell pepper, sliced into ¼" (6mm) strips

2 tablespoons (30ml) chicken stock

2 tablespoons (30ml) cider vinegar

TO ASSEMBLE

4 hoagie or sub rolls, cut to hold the sausage

½ cup (118ml) marinara sauce

Mozzarella cheese

For the Pork Sausage

Preheat a water bath to 140°F (60°C).

Lightly salt and pepper the sausage links, then seal in a sous vide bag. Place the bag in the water bath and cook for 2 to 4 hours until heated through or pasteurized.

For the Peppers and Onions

Heat oil in a pan over medium heat. Add the onions, salt, and pepper it, and cook until it begins to soften, about 10 minutes. Add the garlic and bell pepper and cook for another 5 minutes. Add the chicken stock and vinegar, and mix well. Salt and pepper to taste. Cook until it begins to thicken.

To Assemble

Take the sous vide bag out of the water and remove the cooked Italian sausage. Dry it off thoroughly, using paper towels or a clean dish cloth. Quickly sear the sausage for 1 to 2 minutes per side, just until browned. Remove it from the heat.

Preheat a broiler in the oven.

Brush the cut sides of the hoagie rolls with olive oil and toast under the broiler. Add the sausage, onions, and peppers to the hoagies, then top with the marinara sauce and mozzarella cheese. Melt the cheese under the broiler, then serve.

PORK SHOULDER QUESADILLAS

COOKS: 140°F (60°C) FOR 1 TO 2 DAYS | SERVES: 4

My wife loves quesadillas and I love pork shoulder, so this combination is a favorite of ours. The pork is complemented by cheddar and Monterey Jack cheese, a little diced tomato and jalapeño, as well as some peppery arugula on top. You can vary the fillings and keep it simple with just pork and cheese, or make it as fancy as you like with sautéed onions and peppers. You can also top it with any salsas or sauces you like.

The pork shoulder is cooked at 140°F (60°C), which results in a pork chop–like texture, something that you really can't achieve through traditional cooking. If you prefer your pork shoulder shredded, you can increase the temperature to 165°F (73.9°C) or 176°F (80°C) and reduce the time to 165°F for 18 to 24 Hours (73.9°C) or 176°F for 12 to 18 Hours (80.0°C).

FOR THE PORK SHOULDER

1 teaspoon (5ml) paprika

½ teaspoon (2.5ml) garlic powder

½ teaspoon (2.5ml) ground cumin

½ teaspoon (2.5ml) coriander seeds

½ teaspoon (2.5ml) mustard powder

1–2 pounds (450–900g) pork shoulder

TO ASSEMBLE

8 flour tortillas

Shredded cheddar cheese

Shredded Monterey Jack cheese

1 tomato, diced

1 jalapeño pepper, diced

½ cup (118ml) chopped arugula

1 avocado, sliced

For the Pork Shoulder

Preheat a water bath to 140°F (60°C).

Mix the spices together in a small bowl. Lightly salt and pepper the pork, then sprinkle with the spice mixture. Place the pork in a sous vide bag and seal. Place the bag in the water bath and cook it for 1 to 2 days until tenderized.

To Assemble

Take the sous vide bag out of the water and remove the cooked pork. Dry it off thoroughly, using paper towels or a clean dish cloth. Lightly salt the pork shoulder, then quickly sear it for 1 to 2 minutes per side, just until browned. Remove it from the heat and cut it into strips.

Preheat a grill to high heat or a pan to medium-high heat.

Lay out 4 tortillas and evenly split the steak and other ingredients between them. Top each with a remaining tortilla.

Brush the top of each tortilla with oil and place it on the grill or in the pan. Cover the tortilla while it is cooking. Once it turns golden brown on the bottom, flip it over and continue cooking until the cheese is melted and the quesadilla is browned on both sides. Remove from the heat, cut into quarters, and serve.

PULLED PORK WITH CAROLINA-STYLE MUSTARD-VINEGAR SAUCE

COOKS: 156°F (68.9°C) FOR 18 TO 24 HOURS | SERVES: 4

I was first introduced to real backyard-smoked pulled pork by my friend Sean Rielly. He was from North Carolina and made the process seem so straightforward, with results that were always incredible. But every time I tried it on my own, the pork was never as good as his, which was discouraging, since I had just spent hours monitoring a smoker.

Once I got into sous vide, I started to experiment with pulled pork and this recipe is the one of my favorite ways to make it. It might not be quite as good as Sean's traditionally smoked pork, but I don't have to monitor a smoker all day and it always turns out amazing, which is a big win in my book!

FOR THE PORK SHOULDER

See also Smoked BBQ Brisket (page 32) and Smoked Baby Back Ribs (page 56)

½ teaspoon (2.5ml) garlic powder

½ teaspoon (2.5ml) ground cumin

½ teaspoon ground coriander

⅛ teaspoon (0.5ml) cayenne pepper powder

1–2 pounds (450–900g) pork shoulder

1 tablespoon Worcestershire sauce

1 tablespoon liquid smoke

FOR THE MUSTARD-VINEGAR SAUCE

¾ cup (177ml) prepared yellow mustard

½ cup (118ml) honey

½ cup (118ml) apple cider vinegar

2 tablespoons (30ml) ketchup

1 tablespoon (15ml) brown sugar

1 tablespoon (15ml) Worcestershire sauce

2 teaspoons (10ml) hot sauce

For the Pork Shoulder

Preheat a water bath to 156°F (68.9°C).

Mix the spices together in a bowl. Salt and pepper the pork shoulder, then sprinkle with the spices. Place it in the bag with the Worcestershire sauce and the liquid smoke. Seal the bag, place it in the water bath, and cook for 18 to 24 hours, until tenderized.

For the Mustard-Vinegar Sauce

Whisk together all the ingredients in a bowl.

To Assemble

Take the sous vide bag out of the water and remove the cooked pork. Dry it off thoroughly, using paper towels or a clean dish cloth. Lightly salt the pork shoulder, then quickly sear it for 1 to 2 minutes per side, just until browned. Remove it from the heat and shred.

Serve on rolls with pickles and cabbage, with a spoonful of the mustard-vinegar sauce on top.

TIPS The mustard-vinegar sauce is best when it is made at least a day in advance. It will also last in the refrigerator for at least a week.

If you are comfortable around a smoker, you can omit the liquid smoke and finish the pork in your smoker.

HOISIN-GLAZED SPARE RIBS

COOKS: 140°F (60°C) FOR 1 TO 2 DAYS | SERVES: 4

Spare ribs can sometimes be overly rich and fatty, so I like to pair them with a sweet, spicy, and acidic glaze to help round out the taste. Once the ribs are sous vided, they are brushed with the glaze during the searing process, coating them with flavor and caramelizing the glaze. If you like an even heavier glaze, you can chill the ribs after sous viding them to increase the amount of time they can be seared.

These ribs are cooked at 140°F (60°C), which results in a choplike texture with a lot of bite to it. If you want a more traditional texture, you can raise the temperature between 156°F (68.9°C) and 176°F (80°C) while reducing the sous vide time.

FOR THE PORK SPARE RIBS

- 1 teaspoon (5ml) Chinese five-spice powder
- 1 teaspoon (5ml) garlic powder
- ⅛ teaspoon (0.5ml) cayenne pepper powder
- 1–2 racks pork spare ribs (1¼–2 pounds)

FOR THE HOISIN GLAZE

- ½ cup (118ml) hoisin sauce
- 1 tablespoon (15ml) rice vinegar
- 2 tablespoons (30ml) soy sauce
- 2 tablespoons (30ml) honey
- 1 tablespoon (15ml) fresh lime juice
- 2 teaspoons (10ml) minced ginger
- 2 cloves garlic, minced
- ¼ teaspoon (1ml) cayenne pepper powder

TO ASSEMBLE

- ¼ cup (118ml) chopped fresh cilantro
- 1 teaspoon (5ml) sesame seeds

For the Pork Spare Ribs

Preheat a water bath to 140°F (60°C).

Mix the spices together in a small bowl. Salt and pepper the ribs, then sprinkle with the spices. Place the pork in a sous vide bag and seal it. Place the bag in the water bath and cook for 1 to 2 days until tenderized.

For the Hoisin Glaze

To prepare the glaze, mix together all the ingredients in a bowl until combined well.

To Assemble

Take the sous vide bag out of the water and remove the cooked ribs. Dry them off thoroughly, using paper towels or a clean dish cloth. Lightly salt the spare ribs, then brush with the hoisin glaze. Quickly sear the ribs for 1 minute per side, then add more glaze and sear for another minute. Repeat a few times until the glaze has coated the ribs. Remove the ribs from the heat.

Cut the racks of ribs into sections of 1 or 2 ribs and place them on a plate. Sprinkle with the cilantro and sesame seeds, then serve.

SMOKED BABY BACK RIBS

COOKS: 156°F (68.9°C) FOR 18 TO 24 HOURS | SERVES: 4

When I lived in Connecticut, good BBQ ribs could be hard to find nearby, so I had to resort to making my own. While I love sitting around a smoker for several hours, I don't always have that much time, so I started sous viding them. If you chill them after sous vide, then reheat them on a smoker or a hot grill, the ribs turn out simply amazing, with enough smoke to pass as the real thing.

I prefer my ribs cooked at 156°F (68.9°C) so they are tender and juicy, but still have a little bite to them. If you want them to fall off the bone, you can cook them as high as 176°F (80°C), which also doesn't take as long. For a much firmer rib, I also sometimes like 140°F (60°C). If you don't have access to a smoker or grill, you can just add a teaspoon or two (5–10ml) of liquid smoke to the bag and sear the ribs as you normally sear food.

FOR THE RIBS

½ teaspoon (2.5ml) garlic powder

½ teaspoon (2.5ml) onion powder

½ teaspoon (2.5ml) smoked paprika

¼ teaspoon (1ml) ground coriander

¼ teaspoon (1ml) ground cumin

2–3 pounds (900–1,350g) baby back ribs, membrane removed if desired

For the Ribs

Preheat a water bath to 156°F (68.9°C).

Mix together the spices in a bowl. Lightly salt and pepper the ribs, then sprinkle them with the spices. Place the ribs in a sous vide bag and seal it. Place the bag in the water bath and cook for 18 to 24 hours, until tenderized. Take the sous vide bag out of the water and chill in an ice bath for at least 30 to 60 minutes.

To Assemble

Prepare a smoker to 200°F to 250°F (93.3°C–121.1°C).

Remove the chilled ribs from the sous vide bag and dry them thoroughly, using paper towels or a clean dish cloth. Lightly salt the ribs, then place them in the smoker. Smoke the ribs until the middle reaches 140°F to 150°F (60°C–65.6°C), then remove them from the heat. Cut the ribs into slabs, then serve.

CHAPTER 3

Poultry and Eggs

POULTRY AND EGGS SOUS VIDE

Sous vided poultry is so much more moist and tender than poultry cooked through other methods. This is mainly due to the lower temperatures employed with sous vide. A major concern when cooking chicken and poultry is ensuring that it is safe to eat. Traditionally, this meant cooking chicken to at least 150°F (65.6°C) to 165°F (73.9°C). As we discussed earlier, you can achieve the same safety levels through extended cooking at lower temperatures. This allows you to enjoy much juicier poultry than you normally would.

WHITE MEAT

I prefer my chicken and turkey breasts cooked at 141°F (60.6°C). They are safe as low as 136°F (57.8°C), but then they are a little too raw-tasting for me. Some people like them as high as 147°F (63.9°C), but I find them a little too dry for my taste. At any temperature, they just need to be cooked long enough to be pasteurized, usually 2 to 4 hours, but the actual timing will depend on your desired temperature and the thickness of the food. For more specific times, check out the charts at the back of the book. Using boneless or skinless chicken will not affect the cooking times at all, so use whichever you prefer.

DARK MEAT

Dark meat is usually sous vided from 141°F (60.6°C) up to 156°F (68.9°C) for a tender version, and I personally like 148°F (64.4°C) the best. Dark meat generally doesn't need to be tenderized too much, so the time range is typically 4 to 6 hours.

For shreddable dark meat, the temperature goes much higher, between 160°F (71.1°C) and 176°F (80°C). I usually split the difference and use 165°F (73.9°C). They are cooked longer to allow for more breakdown, usually for 8 to 12 hours.

DUCK AND GOOSE

Duck and goose have more steaklike meat and are often safe when cooked to lower temperatures, even in traditional cooking.

More tender cuts of duck and goose, like the breast, are best cooked just enough to heat them through and pasteurize them at a medium-rare temperature. This normally takes 2 to 3 hours for temperatures from 129°F (53.8°C) to 140°F (60°C). I tend to use 131°F (55°C) when I cook it, though if you prefer medium, you'd probably like it cooked around 140°F (60°C).

CHICKEN BREAST GRAIN BOWL

COOKS: 141°F (60.6°C) FOR 2 TO 4 HOURS | SERVES: 4

When I want to keep my energy up all day, but still eat something hearty and exceptionally tasty, I've found grain bowls to be an amazing option. The combination of sweet vegetables, hearty grains, and some meat or fish, topped with a flavorful sauce makes for a wonderfully filling lunch. You can use any vegetables you have on hand. I'll often use leftovers or just quickly roast some fresh ones in a 400°F (200°C) oven for 20 to 40 minutes.

Sous viding the chicken ensures that it will turn out exceptionally moist and tender. I will often skip the searing step when I'm making this for lunch because, once it is combined with everything else, you barely notice the sear anyway.

FOR THE CHICKEN BREASTS

½ teaspoon (2.5ml) garlic powder

½ teaspoon (2.5ml) ground coriander

¼ teaspoon (1ml) ground cumin

2 chicken breasts

FOR THE LEMON VINAIGRETTE

¼ cup (60ml) olive oil

3 tablespoons (45ml) fresh lemon juice

TO ASSEMBLE

2 cups (473ml) cooked bulgur

2 cups (473ml) mixed cooked vegetables (I prefer squash, carrots, broccoli, and bell peppers)

Fresh parsley

For the Chicken Breasts

Preheat the water bath to 141°F (60.6°C).

Mix together the spices in a bowl. Lightly salt and pepper the chicken breasts, then sprinkle them with the spices. Place the chicken in a sous vide bag and seal it. Place the bag in the water bath and cook the chicken for 2 to 4 hours, until pasteurized.

For the Lemon Vinaigrette

Whisk or blend together the two vinaigrette ingredients, then salt and pepper to taste.

To Assemble

Take the sous vide bag out of the water and remove the cooked chicken breasts from the bag. Dry them off thoroughly, using paper towels or a clean dish cloth. Lightly salt the chicken, then quickly sear it for 1 to 2 minutes per side, just until browned. Remove from the heat and cut the chicken into slices.

To serve, place the bulgur in a bowl and top with the chicken. Add the cooked vegetables and parsley, and drizzle with the lemon vinaigrette.

CHICKEN BREAST WITH LEMON AND PEA FUSILLI

COOKS: 141°F (60.6°C) FOR 2 TO 4 HOURS | SERVES: 4

In this recipe, moist chicken strips top a bright and flavorful lemon and pea pasta for a fast but hearty meal. Once the chicken is cooked, the most time-consuming part of the recipe is boiling the water for the pasta!

I call for fusilli or corkscrew pasta, but you can use anything you have in your pantry. If you want to really elevate this meal, grabbing some fresh pasta is the way to go.

FOR THE CHICKEN BREASTS

2 chicken breasts

4 slices of lemon

2 sprigs fresh rosemary

FOR THE LEMON AND PEA FUSILLI

¼ onion, minced

1 carrot, peeled and diced

3 cloves garlic, minced

2 cups (473ml) frozen peas, thawed

3 cups (710ml) cooked fusilli or corkscrew pasta

2 lemons

TO ASSEMBLE

2 tablespoons (30ml) chopped fresh basil leaves

Parmesan cheese

For the Chicken Breasts

Preheat the water bath to 141°F (60.6°C).

Salt and pepper the chicken breasts and place them in the sous vide bag. Position 2 slices of lemon on each breast, add a rosemary sprig, then seal the bag. Place the bag in the water bath and cook the chicken for 2 to 4 hours, until pasteurized.

For the Lemon and Pea Fusilli

Heat oil in a pan over medium heat. Add the onion and carrot and cook until tender. Add the garlic and cook until fragrant, 2 to 3 minutes. Add the peas and fusilli, and toss to combine, cooking until heated through. Zest the lemons into the pan, then juice them into the pan. Salt and pepper to taste, then remove from the heat.

To Assemble

Take the sous vide bag out of the water and remove the cooked chicken breasts from the bag. Discard the lemon and rosemary. Dry the chicken off thoroughly, using paper towels or a clean dish cloth. Lightly salt the chicken breasts then quickly sear them for 1 to 2 minutes per side, just until browned. Remove from the heat and cut the chicken into slices.

Place the lemon and pea fusilli in a bowl and top with the chicken slices. Sprinkle with the fresh basil, then grate the parmesan cheese on top. Drizzle with olive oil and serve.

TIP I highly recommend getting a hunk of good parmesan cheese and storing it in the refrigerator. It will last for several weeks, if not longer, and you can pull it out and grate some over pasta, stir-fries, soups, and just about anything else you want to add a salty, umami taste to.

CURRIED CHICKEN SALAD

COOKS: 141°F (60.6°C) FOR 2 TO 4 HOURS | SERVES: 4

Chicken salad is often a bland, mayonnaise-heavy mess, but I like to turn it into something amazing with the addition of fruit chutney, sweet grapes, and crunchy apple. Cooking the chicken with sous vide also means it will be moist and flavorful.

I tend to use less dressing than many people, but you can add more or less based on your personal preference. You can use either red or green grapes; just pick whichever ones look the most in season. You can serve the chicken salad as is, over lettuce, or even in a wrap.

FOR THE CHICKEN BREASTS

½ teaspoon (2.5ml) garlic powder

¼ teaspoon (1ml) ground ginger

¼ teaspoon (1ml) ground coriander

¼ teaspoon (1ml) ground cumin

2 chicken breasts

FOR THE CURRY DRESSING

⅓ cup (78ml) mayonnaise

⅓ cup (78ml) fruit chutney

2 tablespoons (30ml) olive oil

1 tablespoon (15ml) fresh lemon juice

2 teaspoons (10ml) curry powder

TO ASSEMBLE

1 celery stalk, diced

2 carrots, peeled and diced

¼ cup (60ml) chopped fresh parsley

¼ cup (60ml) chopped fresh basil leaves

1 cup (237ml) seedless grapes, halved

½ sweet apple, cored and diced

½ cup (118ml) pecans, toasted

For the Chicken Breasts

Preheat the water bath to 141°F (60.6°C).

Mix together the spices in a bowl. Lightly salt and pepper the chicken then sprinkle with the spices. Place the chicken in a sous vide bag and seal. Place the bag in the water bath and cook the chicken for 2 to 4 hours, until pasteurized.

For the Curry Dressing

Whisk together all the dressing ingredients, then salt and pepper to taste.

To Assemble

Take the sous vide bag out of the water and remove the cooked chicken breasts from the bag. Dry them off thoroughly, using paper towels or a clean dish cloth. Lightly salt the chicken, then quickly sear it for 1 to 2 minutes per side, just until browned. Remove from the heat and coarsely chop the chicken into bite-size pieces.

Toss the celery, carrots, parsley, basil, grapes, apples, and chopped chicken together with the curry dressing. Place in a bowl, then top with the pecans and serve.

 TIP Use a good-quality jarred chutney, or make your own using dried or fresh mangoes.

GINGER-SESAME CHICKEN STIR-FRY

COOKS: 141°F (60.6°C) FOR 2 TO 4 HOURS | SERVES: 4

I love Chinese-American food but, unfortunately, it's often filled with overly sweet, sticky sauces. My own take on this restaurant favorite is a light stir-fry of various vegetables, combined with some fish sauce, soy sauce, and rice wine vinegar. You can use any vegetables that appeal to you, but I often turn to onions, peppers, bok choy, snow peas, and carrots. If you want the sauce to be on the heavier side, you can stir in a tablespoon or two (15–30ml) of hoisin sauce or oyster sauce to it. The addition of a minced jalapeño is also a great way to add heat to it.

FOR THE CHICKEN BREASTS

½ teaspoon (2.5ml) garlic powder

½ teaspoon (2.5ml) Chinese five-spice powder

2 chicken breasts

FOR THE VEGETABLE STIR-FRY

1 white onion, diced

1 red bell pepper, sliced

3 cloves garlic, minced

2 tablespoons (30ml) minced ginger

8 baby bok choy

½ pound (225 grams) snow peas

1 cup (237ml) shredded carrots

1 teaspoon (5ml) fish sauce

1 tablespoon (15ml) soy sauce

1 tablespoon (15ml) rice wine vinegar

TO ASSEMBLE

Sesame oil

3 tablespoons (45ml) coarsely chopped peanuts

3 tablespoons (45ml) coarsely chopped fresh cilantro

For the Chicken Breasts

Preheat the water bath to 141°F (60.6°C).

Mix together the spices in a bowl. Lightly salt and pepper the chicken, then sprinkle with the spices. Place the chicken in a sous vide bag and seal. Place the bag in the water bath and cook the chicken for 2 to 4 hours, until pasteurized.

For the Vegetable Stir-Fry

Heat some oil in a pan over medium-high heat. Add the onions and cook until they begin to soften. Add the red pepper, garlic, and ginger, then cook until they start to soften. Add the baby bok choy, snow peas, shredded carrots, fish sauce, soy sauce, and vinegar, then cover and cook until tender.

To Assemble

Take the sous vide bag out of the water and remove the cooked chicken breasts from the bag. Dry them off thoroughly, using paper towels or a clean dish cloth. Lightly salt the chicken, then quickly sear it for 1 to 2 minutes per side, just until browned. Remove from the heat and cut the chicken into slices.

To serve, spoon the vegetable stir-fry onto a plate and top with the chicken. Drizzle with some sesame oil, and sprinkle the chopped peanuts and cilantro on top.

PANKO-FRIED CHICKEN FINGERS

COOKS: 141°F (60.6°C) FOR 2 TO 4 HOURS | SERVES: 4

Chicken fingers are one of my favorite bar snacks, but making them at home always turns into a messy endeavor with the raw chicken, egg coating, and hot oil. Plus, I'm never sure if the chicken is cooked all the way through once the coating is done. Precooking the chicken with sous vide ensures that it is cooked through and will be terrifically moist. In addition, the temperature of the oil isn't as critical as it usually is, since you are just browning the crust, not cooking the chicken.

FOR THE CHICKEN BREASTS

1–2 pounds (450–900g) chicken breasts

FOR THE COATING

2 eggs

¼ cup (60ml) milk

1½ cups (355ml) panko breadcrumbs

½ cup (118ml) grated parmesan cheese

1 teaspoon (5ml) garlic powder

1 teaspoon (5ml) paprika, preferably smoked

⅛ teaspoon (0.5ml) chipotle pepper powder or cayenne pepper powder

TO ASSEMBLE

Oil for frying, preferably peanut, canola, or grapeseed

For the Chicken Breasts

Preheat the water bath to 141°F (60.6°C).

Salt and pepper the chicken, then seal in a sous vide bag. Place the bag in the water bath and cook the chicken for 2 to 4 hours, until pasteurized.

For the Coating

Whisk together the eggs and milk in a bowl. In a separate bowl, combine the remaining ingredients and mix well.

To Assemble

Take the sous vide bag out of the water and remove the cooked chicken breasts from the bag. Dry them off thoroughly, using paper towels or a clean dish cloth, and cut the chicken into slices.

Set a wire rack on a baking sheet over paper towels.

Heat a large pan over medium to medium-high heat. Add enough oil to fill the pan about ¼" (7mm) deep and heat until it is about to smoke.

Working a few strips at a time, place the chicken in the egg and milk mixture, then roll in the panko breadcrumb mixture. Carefully add the chicken to the pan and cook until the side in the oil is browned. Flip the chicken and cook until the pieces are browned all over, then remove them from the heat and set them on the wire rack. Repeat for all the strips.

> **TIP** For a crispier coating, you can briefly chill the chicken breasts in an ice bath for a few minutes before coating and frying them. This will allow you to fry them longer, and thus make them crispier, without overcooking the chicken.

CHICKEN THIGHS WITH CHIMICHURRI

COOKS: 148°F (64.4°C) FOR 4 TO 6 HOURS | SERVES: 4

Every summer I look forward to having fresh herbs from my garden, and even though I live in New York City now, I still keep a few pots of herbs. Over the years, chimichurri has been one of my go-to recipes for using up herbs before they go to waste. Chimichurri is usually very parsley-heavy, but you can add in any herbs you have around; I often improvise with whatever herbs need trimming. The result is always a rich, herb-filled sauce with light heat that can be used on everything from steak to omelets.

For a complete summer meal, I like to finish these chicken thighs on the grill and serve them with some grilled corn or vegetables.

FOR THE CHICKEN THIGHS

- 1 teaspoon (5ml) garlic powder
- ½ teaspoon (2.5ml) paprika
- 1–2 pounds (450–900g) chicken thighs

FOR THE CHIMICHURRI SAUCE

- 2 cups (473ml) chopped fresh parsley
- 2 tablespoons (30ml) fresh oregano leaves
- 6 cloves garlic, coarsely chopped
- 1 tablespoon (15ml) red wine vinegar
- 2 tablespoons (30ml) fresh lime juice
- ½ cup (118ml) olive oil
- 1 teaspoon (5ml) paprika
- ½ jalapeño, seeded and coarsely diced

For the Chicken Thighs

Preheat the water bath to 148°F (64.4°C).

Mix together the spices in a bowl. Lightly salt and pepper the chicken, then sprinkle with the spices. Place the chicken in a sous vide bag and seal. Place the bag in the water bath and cook the chicken for 4 to 6 hours, until pasteurized.

For the Chimichurri Sauce

Combine all the ingredients in a blender or food processor and process until pureed together.

To Assemble

Take the sous vide bag out of the water and remove the cooked chicken thighs from the bag. Dry them off thoroughly, using paper towels or a clean dish cloth. Lightly salt the chicken, then quickly sear it for 1 to 2 minutes per side, just until browned. Remove from the heat.

To serve, spoon the chimichurri sauce on top of the chicken thighs.

CHICKEN THIGHS WITH ROMESCO SAUCE AND ROASTED ASPARAGUS

COOKS: 148°F (64.4°C) FOR 4 TO 6 HOURS | SERVES: 4

I first had romesco sauce a few years ago and it has turned into a favorite of mine. It's a combination of sweet bell peppers, acidic tomatoes, and hearty roasted almonds with light background notes of garlic and a little heat from cayenne pepper. The sauce is especially flavorful when you can find farm-fresh tomatoes and peppers. It is very versatile and can be used on a wide variety of meats or vegetables.

FOR THE CHICKEN THIGHS

1 teaspoon (5ml) ground coriander

1 teaspoon (5ml) garlic powder

1–2 pounds (450–900g) chicken thighs

FOR THE ROASTED ASPARAGUS

1 pound (450g) asparagus, cleaned and trimmed

FOR THE ROMESCO SAUCE

½ cup (118ml) coarsely chopped roasted red bell peppers

3 tomatoes, preferably plum, coarsely chopped

½ cup (118ml) roasted almonds

¼ cup (60ml) fresh parsley

1 tablespoon (15ml) olive oil

½ tablespoon (7.5ml) paprika

¼ teaspoon (1ml) cayenne pepper powder

2 cloves garlic

1 tablespoon (15ml) fresh lemon juice

TO ASSEMBLE

Lemon zest

Fresh parsley

For the Chicken Thighs

Preheat the water bath to 148°F (64.4°C).

Mix together the spices in a bowl. Lightly salt and pepper the chicken, then sprinkle with the spices. Place the thighs in a sous vide bag and seal. Place the bag in the water bath and cook the chicken for 4 to 6 hours, until pasteurized.

For the Roasted Asparagus

Preheat an oven to 400°F (200°C).

Toss the asparagus with olive oil, then salt and pepper it. Place on a rimmed baking sheet, then cook, stirring once or twice, about 15 to 30 minutes or until tender.

For the Romesco Sauce

Place two-thirds of the red peppers and tomatoes into a blender. Add the almonds, parsley, olive oil, paprika, cayenne, garlic, and lemon juice. Blend until relatively smooth. Salt and pepper to taste. Add the remaining red pepper and tomato, then blend until just broken up.

To Assemble

Take the sous vide bag out of the water and remove the cooked chicken thighs from the bag. Dry them off thoroughly, using paper towels or a clean dish cloth. Lightly salt the chicken, then quickly sear it for 1 to 2 minutes per side, just until browned. Remove from the heat.

Place a chicken thigh or two on a plate with the asparagus. Spoon romesco sauce on top and sprinkle with the lemon zest. Top with the parsley, drizzle with olive oil, and serve.

HONEY-HARISSA–MARINATED CHICKEN LEGS AND TOMATO SALAD

COOKS: 148°F (64.4°C) FOR 4 TO 6 HOURS | SERVES: 4

One of my favorite comfort foods is honey BBQ wings, but I don't always have the patience to make them at home. This is my go-to recipe when I want some of that sweet and spicy flavor without having to prep individual wings. If you prefer saucier meat, you can double the amount of sauce and reserve half of it to brush on as a glaze during the searing process. You can also change the ratio of harissa to honey, so it matches the spice level you prefer.

I like to serve these chicken legs with a light tomato salad. It brightens up the meal and complements the spicy chicken.

FOR THE CHICKEN LEGS

3 tablespoons (45ml) harissa or other chili-garlic sauce

1 tablespoon (15ml) soy sauce

1 tablespoon (15ml) honey

1–2 pounds (450–900g) chicken legs

FOR THE TOMATO SALAD

2 cloves garlic, minced

2 tablespoons (30ml) sherry vinegar

3 tablespoons (45ml) olive oil

1 pint (473ml) cherry tomatoes, halved

1 shallot, thinly sliced

½ red bell pepper, cut into thin strips

2 tablespoons (30ml) chopped fresh basil leaves

TO ASSEMBLE

2 tablespoons (30ml) chopped fresh basil leaves

1 teaspoon (15ml) sesame seeds

For the Chicken Legs

Preheat the water bath to 148°F (64.4°C).

Mix the harissa, soy sauce, and honey together. Lightly salt and pepper the chicken, then coat with the honey-harissa mixture. Place the chicken in a sous vide bag and seal. Place the bag in the water bath and cook the chicken for 4 to 6 hours, until pasteurized and tender.

For the Tomato Salad

Place the garlic and vinegar in a bowl and let sit for 5 minutes. While whisking, slowly drizzle in the oil until the mixture comes together. Toss the remaining ingredients with the dressing.

To Assemble

Take the sous vide bag out of the water and remove the cooked chicken legs from the bag. Dry them off thoroughly, using paper towels or a clean dish cloth. Lightly salt the chicken, then quickly sear it for 1 to 2 minutes per side, just until browned. Remove from the heat.

To serve, place a spoonful of the tomato salad on a plate and top with several chicken legs. Sprinkle with the basil and sesame seeds.

CHICKEN CAPRESE GRINDERS

COOKS: 141°F (60.6°C) FOR 2 TO 4 HOURS | SERVES: 4

I love the classic pairing of tomatoes, basil, and mozzarella cheese, especially in the middle of summer when the tomatoes are ripe and plentiful. I use this combination in many different ways, but one of the most versatile is this tomato-basil salsa. With just a splash of balsamic vinegar for sweetness and olive oil for a little richness, it can complement just about any type of meat. Here I use it as a topping for a chicken sausage grinder with melted mozzarella cheese.

Make sure you give the sausage a good sear so the casings have time to firm up; otherwise, they may be chewy.

FOR THE CHICKEN SAUSAGE

1–2 pounds (450–900g) chicken sausages

FOR THE TOMATO-BASIL SALSA

2 tomatoes, diced

¼ cup (60ml) coarsely chopped fresh basil leaves

1 tablespoon (15ml) balsamic vinegar

1 tablespoon (15ml) olive oil

TO ASSEMBLE

4 hoagie or sub rolls, cut to hold the sausage

8 slices of fresh mozzarella rounds, ⅛" (3mm) thick

For the Chicken Sausage

Preheat the water bath to 141°F (60.6°C).

Place the chicken sausage in a sous vide bag and seal. Place the bag in the water bath and cook the chicken for 2 to 4 hours, until pasteurized.

For the Tomato-Basil Salsa

Mix together the tomato, basil, balsamic vinegar, and olive oil in a bowl. Salt and pepper to taste.

To Assemble

Toast the cut sides of the hoagie rolls until they start to brown. Remove from the heat and place the mozzarella cheese on each one.

Take the sous vide bag out of the water and remove the cooked chicken sausages from the bag. Dry them off thoroughly, using paper towels or a clean dish cloth. Quickly sear them until they start to brown, about 3–5 minutes. Remove from the heat.

Place a chicken sausage or two on each roll, then top with the tomato-basil salsa and serve.

DUCK BREAST WITH MANGO SLAW

COOKS: 131°F (55°C) FOR 2 TO 3 HOURS | SERVES: 4

I think the richness of duck breast goes really well with spicy and sweet foods, and this mango slaw fits the bill. It features a combination of crunchy cabbage, sweet mango, and spicy jalapeño that fully rounds out the dish without overwhelming the flavors of the duck.

FOR THE DUCK BREASTS

1–2 pounds (450–900g) duck breasts

FOR THE MANGO SLAW

2 tablespoons (30ml) olive oil

Juice of 1 lime

1 jalapeño, seeded and diced

¼ red onion, diced

1 cup (237ml) shredded red cabbage

1 cup (237ml) shredded green cabbage

1 large mango, peeled and diced

2 tablespoons (30ml) chopped fresh mint

1 teaspoon (5ml) ground cinnamon

TO ASSEMBLE

2 tablespoons (30ml) coarsely chopped fresh cilantro

For the Duck Breasts

Preheat the water bath to 131°F (55°C).

Lightly salt and pepper the duck breasts, then seal them in a sous vide bag. Place the bag in the water bath and cook the duck for 2 to 3 hours, until heated through or pasteurized.

For the Mango Slaw

Place all the mango slaw ingredients in a bowl and mix well.

To Assemble

Take the sous vide bag out of the water and remove the cooked duck breasts from the bag. Dry them off thoroughly, using paper towels or a clean dish cloth. Lightly salt the duck breasts, then quickly sear them until the outside has browned and the fat has begun to render. Remove from the heat and cut the duck into slices.

To serve, place several slices of duck on a plate and top with the mango slaw. Sprinkle with the cilantro and drizzle with olive oil.

> **TIP** When searing a duck breast, you can go longer than you expect on the fat side. You want to make sure you render a decent amount of the fat, so the sear on that side will generally not be as quick as most post–sous vide sears.

DUCK BREAST WITH ROASTED MUSHROOMS

COOKS: 131°F (55°C) FOR 2 TO 3 HOURS | SERVES: 4

I usually save duck breasts for fancy dinners, but every once in a while I get inspired to make them on a week-night. Pairing them with this simple roasted-mushroom-and-pepper side is a fantastic way to put together a fast meal in no time. I'll often round it out with some cooked farro or bulgur that will help fuel me through the rest of the week. You can also add any quick-cooking vegetables to the mushrooms and peppers: I often toss in zucchini, eggplant, asparagus, or green beans.

FOR THE DUCK BREASTS

1–2 pounds (450–900g) duck breasts

1 teaspoon (5ml) Chinese five-spice powder

FOR THE ROASTED MUSHROOMS AND PEPPERS

1 pound (450g) baby bella mushrooms, cleaned and trimmed

1 onion, coarsely chopped

2 red or yellow bell peppers, coarsely chopped

TO ASSEMBLE

2 tablespoons (30ml) chopped fresh basil leaves

1 tablespoon (15ml) fresh oregano leaves

For the Duck Breasts

Preheat the water bath to 131°F (55°C).

Lightly salt and pepper the duck breasts, then sprinkle them with the Chinese five-spice powder. Place the duck breasts in a sous vide bag and seal. Place the bag in the water bath and cook the duck for 2 to 3 hours, until heated through or pasteurized.

For the Roasted Mushrooms and Peppers

Preheat an oven to 400°F (200°C).

Toss the mushrooms, onions, and bell peppers with olive oil, then salt and pepper them. Place on a rimmed baking sheet, then cook, stirring once or twice, about 20 to 40 minutes or until tender.

To Assemble

Take the sous vide bag out of the water and remove the cooked duck breasts from the bag. Dry them off thoroughly, using paper towels or a clean dish cloth. Lightly salt the duck, then quickly sear it until the outside has browned and the fat has begun to render. Remove from the heat and cut the duck into slices.

Place a spoonful or two of the roasted mushrooms and peppers on a plate and top with several slices of the duck breast. Sprinkle with the basil and oregano leaves, then serve.

DUCK BREAST WITH SWEET POTATO AND CORN SALAD

COOKS: 131°F (55°C) FOR 2 TO 3 HOURS | SERVES: 4

My wife loves sweet potatoes and duck, so this is one of her favorite recipes. The duck always comes out perfectly cooked with hints of the spice, while the sweet potato and corn salad is bursting with flavor. It combines tasty sweet potatoes and spicy poblano pepper with corn kernels contributing bursts of sweetness, all rounded out with black-eyed peas to bulk up the meal. The sauce mainly comes from the cooked vegetables with a little extra apple cider vinegar to brighten it all up.

FOR THE DUCK BREASTS

⅛ teaspoon (0.5ml) ground cumin

⅛ teaspoon (0.5ml) ground cloves

Pinch of ground nutmeg

1–2 pounds (450–900g) duck breasts

FOR THE SWEET POTATO AND CORN SALAD

¼ red onion, finely diced

1 sweet potato, diced

2 tablespoons (30ml) minced poblano pepper, or jalapeño pepper

3 cloves garlic, minced

½ teaspoon (2.5ml) paprika

½ teaspoon (2.5ml) ancho pepper powder or another chili powder

1 cup (237 ml) cooked corn kernels

1 cup (237 ml) cooked black-eyed peas

1 tablespoon (15ml) apple cider vinegar

¼ cup (60ml) minced fresh cilantro

TO ASSEMBLE

1 cup (237 ml) microgreens or sprouts

For the Duck Breasts

Preheat the water bath to 131°F (55°C).

Mix together the spices in a bowl. Lightly salt and pepper the duck, then sprinkle with the spices. Place the duck breasts in a sous vide bag and seal. Place the bag in the water bath and cook the duck for 2 to 3 hours, until heated through or pasteurized.

For the Sweet Potato and Corn Salad

Heat some olive oil in a pan over medium heat. Add the red onion and cook for 5 minutes. Add the sweet potato and cook until tender, stirring occasionally, about 8 minutes. Add the poblano pepper, garlic, paprika, and ancho pepper powder, and cook until the poblano pepper is tender, about 4 minutes. Stir in the corn, peas, and cider vinegar, and heat thoroughly. Stir in the cilantro, then season with salt and pepper.

To Assemble

Take the sous vide bag out of the water and remove the duck breasts from the bag. Dry them off thoroughly, using paper towels or a clean dish cloth. Lightly salt the duck, then quickly sear it until the outside has browned and the fat has begun to render. Remove from the heat and cut the duck into slices.

To serve, place a spoonful or two of the sweet potato and corn salad on a plate or in a bowl, and top with several slices of the duck. Drizzle with olive oil, then sprinkle the microgreens on top.

TURKEY CLUB SANDWICHES

COOKS: 141°F (60.6°C) FOR 2 TO 4 HOURS | SERVES: 4

Turkey clubs are my mom's favorite sandwich, and she orders them whenever we go to a diner or deli. They are also really easy to make at home, and using sous vided turkey ensures that they will be moist and delicious. This recipe is for a classic club sandwich, but if you wanted to add cheese, use mustard, or put it on a hoagie roll instead of bread, I won't tell!

FOR THE TURKEY BREAST

1–2 pounds (450–900g) turkey breast

TO ASSEMBLE

12 slices of high-quality bread, toasted

Mayonnaise

8 large lettuce leaves

4 slices tomato

8 strips cooked bacon

16 toothpicks

For the Turkey Breast

Preheat the water bath to 141°F (60.6°C).

Salt and pepper the turkey then seal in a sous vide bag. Place the bag in the water bath and cook the turkey for 2 to 4 hours, until pasteurized.

To Assemble

Take the sous vide bag out of the water and remove the cooked turkey from the bag. Dry it off thoroughly, using paper towels or a clean dish cloth. Lightly salt the turkey, then quickly sear it for 1 to 2 minutes per side, just until browned. Remove from the heat and cut the turkey into thin slices.

For each club sandwich, take a piece of bread and spread mayonnaise on one side. Add several slices of turkey to the bread and top with a piece of lettuce. Add another piece of bread and top with a slice of tomato, a piece of lettuce, and 2 strips of bacon. Spread mayonnaise on another piece of bread and place that on top of the sandwich. Cut the sandwich into quarters and place a toothpick through each quarter to hold it together.

Repeat for the remaining 3 sandwiches, then serve.

TURKEY BREAST WITH TABBOULEH

COOKS: 141°F (60.6°C) FOR 2 TO 4 HOURS | SERVES: 4

When I'm in the mood for a light but tasty meal, I often use tabbouleh as a base. This herb-heavy salad with tomatoes and bulgur, regularly used in Middle Eastern cooking, comes together very quickly and has a complex mixture of flavors that go perfectly with simple turkey breasts. You can eat any leftover tabbouleh on lettuce or with warm pitas as a meal of its own.

FOR THE TURKEY BREAST

1 teaspoon (5ml) paprika

¼ teaspoon (1ml) ground ginger

¼ teaspoon (1ml) ground cumin

⅛ teaspoon (0.5ml) ground cloves

⅛ teaspoon (0.5ml) ground cinnamon

1 bay leaf, finely crumbled

1–2 pounds (450–900g) turkey breast

FOR THE TABBOULEH SALAD

3 cups (710ml) well-dried and finely chopped fresh flat-leaf parsley

1 cup (237ml) well-dried and finely chopped fresh mint

½ cup (118ml) cooked/hydrated bulgur, well drained

2 medium tomatoes, diced

2 tablespoons (30ml) fresh lemon juice

⅛ sweet onion, minced

3 tablespoons (45ml) olive oil

TO ASSEMBLE

Fresh mint leaves

For the Turkey Breast

Preheat the water bath to 141°F (60.6°C).

Mix together the spices in a bowl. Lightly salt and pepper the turkey, then sprinkle with the spices. Place the turkey breast in a sous vide bag and seal. Place the bag in the water bath and cook the turkey for 2 to 4 hours, until pasteurized.

For the Tabbouleh Salad

Mix together all the ingredients in a large bowl.

To Assemble

Take the sous vide bag out of the water and remove the cooked turkey from the bag. Dry it off thoroughly, using paper towels or a clean dish cloth. Lightly salt the turkey, then quickly sear it for 1 to 2 minutes per side, just until browned. Remove from the heat and cut the turkey into slices.

Place some turkey slices on a plate and top with the tabbouleh salad. Add some fresh mint leaves and serve.

OPEN-FACED TURKEY THIGH SANDWICHES WITH SAGE GRAVY

COOKS: 148°F (64.4°C) FOR 4 TO 6 HOURS | SERVES: 4

Sandwiches like these always remind me of eating Thanksgiving leftovers, but I tend to enjoy them more when I didn't just eat a ton of turkey the day before. This is also a quick recipe that results in a rich and flavorful meal, making it a great choice for a weeknight when you just want something satisfying without loads of effort. The sage gravy is wonderfully aromatic, and complements Thanksgiving dinner as well.

FOR THE TURKEY THIGHS

1–2 pounds (450–900g) turkey thighs

FOR THE SAGE GRAVY

4 tablespoons (60ml) butter

3 tablespoons (45ml) flour

2 cups (473ml) turkey stock or chicken stock

10 fresh sage leaves, minced

TO ASSEMBLE

4 slices of bread

4 fresh sage leaves, minced

For the Turkey Thighs

Preheat the water bath to 148°F (64.4°C).

Lightly salt and pepper the turkey, then seal in a sous vide bag. Place the bag in the water bath and cook the turkey for 4 to 6 hours, until pasteurized and tender.

For the Sage Gravy

In a large skillet or saucepan over medium heat, melt the butter. Once the butter stops frothing, add the flour and mix until it forms a paste. Incorporate the turkey stock and sage by whisking to combine with the flour paste. Bring to a boil and then remove from the heat. Salt and pepper to taste.

To Assemble

Take the sous vide bag out of the water and remove the cooked turkey from the bag. Dry it off thoroughly, using paper towels or a clean dish cloth. Lightly salt the turkey, then quickly sear it for 1 to 2 minutes per side, just until browned. Remove from the heat and cut the turkey into slices.

Place a piece of bread on a plate and top with several slices of turkey. Spoon some gravy over the top, sprinkle with the sage leaves, and serve.

TURKEY THIGHS WITH CRANBERRY CHUTNEY

COOKS: 148°F (64.4°C) FOR 4 TO 6 HOURS | SERVES: 4

If you live in the United States, I don't have to explain to you that turkey and cranberries go together—since you've probably been eating them on Thanksgiving your entire life! This is my take on the traditional canned cranberry sauce. Putting it together is easier than it looks and it has a whole lot more flavor than what comes out of a can. Here I pair it with turkey thighs, but it goes equally well with turkey breasts, and I'll even use it as a spread on a turkey sandwich.

FOR THE TURKEY THIGHS

1–2 pounds (450–900g) turkey
   thighs

FOR THE CRANBERRY CHUTNEY

3½ cups (828ml) cranberries

1 cup (237ml) fresh orange juice

½ cup (118ml) water

⅓ cup (78ml) brown sugar

½ cup (118ml) granulated sugar

1 dried ancho or chipotle pepper

1 teaspoon (5ml) diced fresh ginger

⅓ cup (78ml) triple sec or Grand
   Marnier

¾ teaspoon (3ml) ground cinnamon

½ teaspoon (2.5ml) ground cloves

For the Turkey Thighs

Preheat the water bath to 148°F (64.4°C).

Lightly salt and pepper the turkey thighs, then place them in a sous vide bag and seal. Place the bag in the water bath and cook the turkey for 4 to 6 hours, until pasteurized and tender.

For the Cranberry Chutney

Combine the cranberries, orange juice, water, brown sugar, granulated sugar, ancho pepper, and ginger in a medium-sized pot. Bring to a simmer and let the mixture cook until the cranberries have released their juices, about 20 minutes. Remove the pot from the heat and discard the ancho pepper.

Add the triple sec, cinnamon, and cloves, then blend well using a blender or food processor. You want the chutney to bind together but still have chunks of cranberry in it.

To Assemble

Take the sous vide bag out of the water and remove the turkey thighs from the bag. Dry them off thoroughly, using paper towels or a clean dish cloth. Lightly salt the turkey, then quickly sear it for 1 to 2 minutes per side, just until browned. Remove from the heat and cut the turkey into slices.

To serve, place several slices of turkey on a plate and top with the cranberry chutney.

 TIP The cranberry chutney will last for about a week in the refrigerator, and can be served cold or reheated.

CHIPOTLE-MARINATED TURKEY LEG

COOKS: 148°F (64.4°C) FOR 3 TO 6 HOURS | SERVES: 4

Nothing says summer BBQ fun like gnawing on a giant grilled turkey leg! Most turkey legs are smoked for several hours, but I usually don't have the patience for that, so I'll cook them in the sous vide machine and then finish them off on the grill or under the broiler. I like to use this chipotle marinade to infuse the meat with lots of amazing flavors, and to spread on the turkey after it is done searing. If you're not serving this as a party food, you'll want to pair it with some vegetables or a salad.

FOR THE CHIPOTLE MARINADE

3 roma tomatoes

4 cloves garlic, peeled

½ onion, coarsely chopped

½ cup (118ml) fresh lime juice

3 tablespoons (45ml) fresh orange juice

2 tablespoons (30ml) apple cider or red wine vinegar

3 canned chipotles in adobo sauce

1 teaspoon (5ml) dried oregano

½ teaspoon (2.5ml) ground cumin

½ teaspoon (2.5ml) ground coriander

FOR THE TURKEY LEG

1–2 pounds (450–900g) turkey leg

For the Chipotle Marinade

Place all the ingredients in a blender or food processor and process into a thick puree.

For the Turkey Leg

Preheat the water bath to 148°F (64.4°C).

Lightly salt and pepper the turkey leg, then place it in a sous vide bag and pour half the marinade in the bag. Reserve the rest of the marinade and place it in the refrigerator. Seal the bag, then place it in the water bath and cook the turkey for 3 to 6 hours, until pasteurized and tender.

To Assemble

Take the sous vide bag out of the water and remove the turkey leg from the bag. Dry it off thoroughly, using paper towels or a clean dish cloth. Lightly salt the turkey, then quickly sear it for 1 to 2 minutes per side, just until browned. Remove from the heat.

Serve with a spoonful of the reserved marinade on top.

> **TIP** I usually use a Ziploc freezer bag to seal the turkey legs because otherwise the marinade will get sucked out of the bag and into my vacuum sealer.

TURKEY BURGER WITH AVOCADO AND BACON

COOKS: 141°F (60.6°C) FOR 2 TO 4 HOURS | SERVES: 4

If you are looking for a lighter take on "burger night," then these turkey burgers should do the trick. The patties are seasoned with garlic, onion, and paprika with a little bit of dried basil added in. I'll often toss in some chipotle or cayenne chili powder if I'm in the mood for some spice. They are finished off with creamy avocado, tangy Swiss cheese, and smoky bacon. For additional flavor, I like to pan-fry the buns in the same pan I've used to sear the patties, so they pick up some of those great browned bits.

FOR THE TURKEY PATTIES

½ teaspoon (2.5ml) garlic powder

½ teaspoon (2.5ml) onion powder

½ teaspoon (2.5ml) paprika, preferably smoked

½ teaspoon (2.5ml) dried basil

4 ground turkey patties, about 4 ounces (113g) each

TO ASSEMBLE

4 hamburger buns

4 slices Swiss cheese

1 avocado, sliced

8 strips cooked bacon

For the Turkey Patties

Preheat the water bath to 141°F (60.6°C).

Mix together the spices in a bowl. Lightly salt and pepper the turkey patties, then sprinkle with the spices. Place the turkey patties in a sous vide bag and seal. Place the bag in the water bath and cook the turkey patties for 2 to 4 hours, until pasteurized.

To Assemble

Take the sous vide bag out of the water and remove the turkey patties from the bag. Dry them off thoroughly, using paper towels or a clean dish cloth. Lightly salt the turkey, then quickly sear it for 1 to 2 minutes per side, just until browned. Remove from the heat.

To serve, place each turkey patty on a bun, then top with Swiss cheese, avocado, and bacon.

CHEDDAR CHEESE–EGG CUP WITH CORN, ONION, AND RED PEPPER

COOKS: 170°F (76.6°C) FOR 1 HOUR | SERVES: 4

When Starbucks started carrying sous vide egg cup bites, the sous vide community quickly jumped to create their own recipes. They are basically a portable omelet in a jar that you can eat on the go. They even store well in the refrigerator so you can make a big batch ahead of time and grab them for a quick breakfast.

This version is very vegetable-heavy, with corn, onion, and red pepper mixed into the eggs and some cheddar cheese to tie it all together.

FOR THE EGGS

6 eggs

½ cup (118ml) shredded cheddar cheese

½ cup (118ml) heavy cream

½ cup (118ml) cooked corn kernels

½ cup (118ml) cooked diced onion

½ cup (118ml) cooked diced red pepper

For the Eggs

Preheat a water bath to 170°F (76.6°C).

Whisk or blend together the eggs, cheese, cream, and salt and pepper to taste. Evenly distribute the remaining ingredients among four canning jars. Add the egg mixture evenly to the jars, then screw the lid on the jar until it's finger-tight, basically until you feel medium resistance when tightening, using only your fingertips. This will allow some air to escape during the sous vide process and help prevent breakage.

Shake the jars well so the ingredients will combine. Place in the water bath and cook for 60 minutes.

Remove from the water bath and run a knife along the inside of the jar to loosen each egg, then invert onto individual plates and serve.

> **TIP** You can make them in any glass container but the ¼ pint (118ml) or ½ pint (237ml) canning jars work really well. Just make sure to only finger-tighten the lid so the gases can escape. I've also made them in ramekins, which create a great shape for the egg.

MUSHROOM, SPINACH, AND GRUYÈRE EGG CUP

COOKS: 170°F (76.6°C) FOR 1 HOUR | SERVES: 4

Mushroom, spinach, and Gruyère—a classic trio—make for a wonderful egg cup bite. Make sure you cook the spinach and mushrooms ahead of time; otherwise, they tend to release a lot of water, which prevents the egg from properly binding. It will still taste fine; it just will have a watery texture.

FOR THE EGGS

6 eggs

½ cup (118ml) shredded Gruyère cheese

½ cup (118ml) heavy cream

½ cup (118ml) cooked, sliced mushrooms

½ cup (118ml) cooked spinach

For the Eggs

Preheat a water bath to 170°F (76.6°C).

Whisk or blend together the eggs, cheese, cream, and salt and pepper to taste. Evenly distribute the remaining ingredients among four canning jars. Add the egg mixture evenly to the jars, then screw the lids on the jars until finger-tight, basically until you feel medium resistance when tightening using only your fingertips. This will allow some air to escape during the sous vide process and help prevent breakage. Shake the jars well so the ingredients will combine. Place in the water bath and cook for 60 minutes.

Remove from the water bath and run a knife along the inside of the jar to loosen each egg, then invert onto individual plates and serve.

> TIP For a lighter egg, you can replace the cream with milk or use ¼ cup (60ml) of cream cheese for a denser end result. You can even make an egg-white-only version.

AVOCADO TOAST WITH POACHED EGG

COOKS: 145°F (62.8°C) FOR 45 MINUTES | SERVES: 4

Poached eggs can be difficult to make with sous vide, and many people actually prefer the traditional method, but for those adventurous people out there, here's how it's done. For best results it is a two-step process. The eggs are first boiled, in their shells, for a minute or two to set the outside of the egg white. Then they are sous vided at a much lower temperature to cook the eggs through to the middle while still keeping them creamy. I like to cook them at 145°F (62.8°C) but you can go a few degrees higher or lower, depending on the consistency you prefer for egg yolks.

FOR THE EGGS
4 eggs

FOR THE AVOCADO SPREAD
2 avocados
2 tablespoons (30ml) olive oil
Fresh lime juice

TO ASSEMBLE
4 slices whole grain bread, toasted
Fresh basil leaves, chopped
Freshly cracked black pepper
Sea salt

For the Eggs

Preheat a water bath to 145°F (62.8°C). Bring a pot of water to a boil on the stovetop. Prepare an ice bath with half ice and half water.

Gently place the eggs in the boiling water and cook for 3 minutes. Remove from the boiling water and place in the ice bath for 1 to 2 minutes, then transfer to the water bath. Let the eggs cook for 45 minutes. Once cooked, remove them from the water bath.

For the Avocado Spread

Peel and remove the flesh from the avocado, and mash together with the olive oil. Add the lime juice, and salt and pepper to taste, until the spread is slightly tangy and well balanced.

To Assemble

Take a slice of toasted bread and slather on some of the avocado spread. Crack a poached egg on top then sprinkle with the basil, fresh cracked pepper, and sea salt.

CHAPTER 4

Fish and Shellfish

FISH AND SHELLFISH SOUS VIDE

Sous vide does an amazing job elevating the flavors and textures of poached or steamed fish, but tends to be less successful in replicating pan-fried preparations. With the precision temperature controls, you have a wide range of cooking temperatures, resulting in many different textures.

The lowest temperature most people use is 104°F (40°C) to 110°F (43.3°C). This just slightly heats the fish through, releasing some flavor, but not significantly changing the texture. This fish is almost sashimi-like.

From 110°F (43.3°C) to 120°F (48.9°C), the fish generally begins to exhibit more pronounced texture changes, becoming slightly more flaky and firm, while still retaining a lot of moisture.

At temperatures above 120°F (48.9°C), the fish starts to become more and more flaky and begins to dry out. The top temperature I usually cook any fish at is 132°F (55.5°C), though some people like it up to 140°F (60°C).

Fish is almost always just heated through, so the cooking time is based on the thickness of the fish. There are some shellfish that do need to be tenderized. Specific recommendations can be found in the charts on page 164.

SOUS VIDE FISH TIPS

Unless you are heating your fish above 130°F (54.4°C) for an extended time, which rarely is the case, be sure to only use fish that you would feel safe eating raw and do not serve it to immunodeficient people.

This is true not only of sousvided fish, but also of fish cooked in a traditional manner.

It is usually best to brine fish. It will help firm it up and will also pull out the albumin, resulting in a cleaner finished dish. Either a wet or dry brine can be used, but I usually use a dry brine. Just salt the fish and refrigerate it for at least 30 minutes before sous viding.

It is generally best to portion out the fish before you sous vide it. Most fish becomes very delicate once it's sous vided, so cutting it into portions first makes it much easier to handle. Sometimes it is also easiest to cut the sous vide bag off the fish, rather than trying to remove the fish with tongs or a spatula.

If you are cooking more than one piece of fish in the same bag, it is usually best to add some olive oil or butter. This will help prevent the pieces from sticking together.

The flesh of fish is generally soft, so be careful when vacuum sealing. A strong vacuum can crush the fish and change the texture. I often use Ziploc bags with fish because they place no added pressure on the fish itself.

Depending on your dish, you can often skip the searing step, or only sear on one side. This is usually true for "poached" preparations, where you want to keep the flavor and texture delicate, as well as many of the low-temperature cooks.

You can leave the skin on or take it off, as it doesn't affect the cooking time much, but be sure to sear on that side to crisp it up slightly.

SWORDFISH WITH ROASTED CAULIFLOWER SALAD

COOKS: 130°F (54.4°C) FOR 15 TO 45 MINUTES | SERVES: 4

Swordfish is my wife's favorite fish, but she almost never orders it out anymore because most restaurants can't make it as well as I can. My secret? Sous vide it and serve it! It only takes about 45 minutes from start to finish and it always has a melt-in-your-mouth texture and buttery flavor. I sometimes sear it once it is sous vided, but, honestly, it is great even without a sear.

The cauliflower salad contributes some much-needed crunch to the dish, along with some acidity from the tomatoes and vinegar.

FOR THE SWORDFISH

4 swordfish portions, about 6 ounces (170g) each

2 tablespoons (30ml) butter or olive oil

FOR THE ROASTED CAULIFLOWER SALAD

1 head of cauliflower, chopped into florets

1 red bell pepper, chopped

1 teaspoon (5ml) fresh thyme leaves

2 tablespoons (30ml) olive oil

10 cherry tomatoes, halved

2 tablespoons (30ml) sherry vinegar

2 tablespoons (30ml) chopped fresh basil leaves

TO ASSEMBLE

Watercress or microgreens

For the Swordfish

Preheat the water bath to 130°F (54.4°C).

Salt and pepper the fish, place in the sous vide bag with the butter, and seal. Let the fish sit for 30 minutes for the dry brine to take effect. Place the bag in the water bath and cook the fish for 15 to 45 minutes, until heated through.

For the Roasted Cauliflower Salad

Preheat an oven to 400°F (200°C).

Toss the cauliflower and red pepper with the thyme leaves and olive oil, then salt and pepper them. Place them on a rimmed baking sheet in a single layer. Roast the cauliflower mixture until tender, 20 to 30 minutes, stirring occasionally. Remove from the heat and toss with the cherry tomatoes, vinegar, and basil. Salt and pepper to taste.

To Assemble

Take the sous vide bag out of the water and remove the cooked fish from the bag. Dry it off thoroughly, using paper towels or a clean dish cloth. Lightly salt the fish, then quickly sear one side until it starts to brown. Remove from the heat.

Place the cauliflower salad on a plate and add the swordfish, browned side up. Top with the watercress and serve.

HALIBUT WITH CUCUMBER AND RED ONION SALAD

COOKS: 120°F (48.9°C) FOR 15 TO 45 MINUTES | SERVES: 4

Halibut dries out easily using traditional cooking methods, which is why sous viding it can make such a difference. In this recipe I cook it at a lower temperature and chill it, resulting in an almost sashimi-like texture. If you want flakier halibut, you can increase the temperature to 130°F (54.4°C). I serve the chilled halibut with a crisp salad of pickled red onion, cucumber, bell peppers, and apple topped with a citrusy orange vinaigrette.

FOR THE HALIBUT

4 halibut portions, about 6 ounces (170g) each

2 tablespoons (30ml) butter or olive oil

FOR THE PICKLED RED ONION

¼ red onion, thinly sliced

½ cup (118ml) white wine vinegar

½ cup (118ml) water

3 tablespoons (45ml) sugar

FOR THE SALTED CUCUMBER

2 mini cucumbers or 1 medium cucumber, thinly sliced

FOR THE ORANGE VINAIGRETTE

¼ cup (60ml) olive oil

3 tablespoons (45ml) fresh orange juice

TO ASSEMBLE

1 yellow bell pepper, thinly sliced

1 Granny Smith apple, cored and diced

Sunflower shoots or other microgreens

For the Halibut

Preheat the water bath to 120°F (48.9°C).

Salt and pepper the fish, and place in the sous vide bag with the butter. Seal the bag. Let the fish sit for 30 minutes for the dry brine to take effect. Place the bag in the water bath and cook the fish for 15 to 45 minutes, until heated through.

Once the fish is cooked, remove the sous vide bag from the water bath and place in a bath of ice water to chill.

For the Pickled Red Onion

Place the onions, white wine vinegar, water, and sugar in a pot and bring to a boil. Reduce the heat and let the mixture simmer for 5 minutes. Remove from the heat and let cool completely.

For the Salted Cucumber

Place the cucumber rounds in a colander and toss them with salt. Let them sit for at least 10 to 15 minutes.

For the Orange Vinaigrette

Whisk or blend together all the vinaigrette ingredients, then salt and pepper to taste.

To Assemble

Remove the halibut from the bag. Dry it off thoroughly, using paper towels or a clean dish cloth.

Pile the pickled red onions, cucumbers, yellow peppers, and apples on a plate. Place the halibut on the vegetables. Top it with the sunflower shoots, drizzle with the vinaigrette, then serve.

SOUS VIDE COD WITH SAUTÉED VEGETABLES

COOKS: 130°F (54.4°C) FOR 15 TO 45 MINUTES | SERVES: 4

When I was living in Connecticut I could always find cod at the fish market, but I could only eat seafood chowder and fish and chips so many times before I needed a break. This vegetable stir-fry was a great way to break up the monotony and enjoy the cod as the star of the dish. Below are some suggested vegetables that work well with cod, but you can use whatever vegetables you have on hand.

FOR THE COD

4 cod portions, about 6 ounces (170g) each

4 slices of lemon

2 tablespoons (30ml) butter or olive oil

FOR THE SAUTÉED VEGETABLES

½ pound (225g) green beans, cleaned and ends trimmed

¼ pound (113g) shiitake mushrooms, cut into strips

1 red bell pepper, cut into strips

3 carrots, peeled and diced

1 tablespoon (15ml) sherry vinegar

1 tablespoon (15ml) olive oil

TO ASSEMBLE

Fresh basil leaves, chopped

Juice of 1 lemon

For the Cod

Preheat the water bath to 130°F (54.4°C).

Salt and pepper the fish, and place in the sous vide bag. Position a slice of lemon on each piece, add the butter, then seal the bag. Let the fish sit for 30 minutes for the dry brine to take effect. Place the bag in the water bath and cook the fish for 15 to 45 minutes, until heated through.

For the Sautéed Vegetables

Working with each vegetable individually, heat some oil in a pan over medium heat, add the vegetable, and cook until tender, stirring occasionally. Remove from the heat.

Once the vegetables are all tender, combine them in a bowl with the sherry vinegar and olive oil. Season with salt and pepper.

To Assemble

Take the sous vide bag out of the water and remove the cooked fish from the bag. Dry it off thoroughly, using paper towels or a clean dish cloth. Lightly salt the fish, then quickly sear one side until it starts to brown. Remove from the heat.

To serve, place the sautéed vegetables in a bowl and top with the cod. Add some basil leaves and squeeze some lemon juice on top. Season with salt.

TUNA SASHIMI

COOKS: 110°F (43.3°C) FOR 15 TO 45 MINUTES | SERVES: 4 AS AN APPETIZER

This recipe is a delightful take on warm tuna sashimi as an appetizer. The tuna is lightly cured with soy sauce and fish sauce, then cooks at a very low 110°F (43.3°C), just warming it through and slightly firming up the flesh. It is then thinly sliced and served with a variety of toppings that contribute crisp texture and bright flavors. I often use salmon in this recipe and equally great results.

FOR THE TUNA

1 tablespoon (15ml) soy sauce

1 teaspoon (5ml) fish sauce

½ pound (225g) sashimi-grade tuna

TO ASSEMBLE

1 radish, thinly sliced

1 avocado, peeled, pitted, and cut into strips

1 teaspoon (5ml) sesame oil

1 teaspoon (5ml) sesame seeds, roasted

1 scallion, thinly sliced

1 lime, cut into eighths

For the Tuna

Preheat the water bath to 110°F (43.3°C).

Mix the soy sauce and fish sauce together to form a wet brine. Pepper the tuna, then brush liberally with the wet brine. Place in the sous vide bag and lightly seal. Let the fish sit for 30 minutes for the brine to take effect. Then place the bag in the water bath and cook for 15 to 45 minutes, until heated through.

To Assemble

Take the sous vide bag out of the water and remove the cooked fish from the bag. Dry it off thoroughly, using paper towels or a dish cloth, then cut into ¼" (7mm) slices.

Place some of the radish slices on a plate and top with the tuna. Top with some avocado strips and drizzle the sesame oil on top. Sprinkle with the sesame seeds and scallions. Serve with the lime wedges.

FLOUNDER WITH CUCUMBER AND TOMATO SALAD

COOKS: 130°F (54.4°C) FOR 15 TO 45 MINUTES | SERVES: 4

Flounder has a mild and sweet flavor with a delicate texture. I prefer to serve it with something that adds a crunch, such as this cucumber and tomato salad. The flavor of the salad is rounded out with some dill, capers, and a splash of sweet balsamic vinegar.

Flounder is very delicate, so it can be hard to sear without having it falling apart. Feel free to skip the searing step, if you prefer.

FOR THE FLOUNDER

4 flounder portions, about 6 ounces (170g) each

2 tablespoons (30ml) butter or olive oil

FOR THE CUCUMBER AND TOMATO SALAD

1 cucumber, seeded and diced

3 tablespoons (45ml) chopped fresh dill

1 teaspoon (5ml) capers

12–15 cherry tomatoes, halved

1 tablespoon (15ml) balsamic vinegar

2 tablespoons (30ml) olive oil

TO ASSEMBLE

2 tablespoons (30ml) chopped fresh basil leaves

Sea salt

For the Flounder

Preheat the water bath to 130°F (54.4°C).

Salt and pepper the fish and place in the sous vide bag with the butter, then seal the bag. Let the fish sit for 30 minutes for the dry brine to take effect. Place the bag in the water bath and cook the fish for 15 to 45 minutes, until heated through.

For the Cucumber and Tomato Salad

Place all the ingredients in a bowl and stir to thoroughly combine.

To Assemble

Take the sous vide bag out of the water and remove the cooked fish from the bag. Dry it off thoroughly, using paper towels or a clean dish cloth. Lightly salt the fish, then quickly sear one side until it starts to brown. Remove from the heat.

Place the flounder on a plate, browned side up, and top with a spoonful or two of the salad. Sprinkle with the basil and sea salt, and serve.

RED SNAPPER POKE BOWL

COOKS: 110°F (43.3°C) FOR 15 TO 45 MINUTES | SERVES: 4

Many poke bowls are served cold, but I think heating red snapper at a low temperature allows more of the flavor to come through. It also firms up the fish, giving it a more appealing texture. Be sure to use high-quality fish because you are still eating it raw. This also works well with tuna, salmon, or other common sushi fish. Feel free to use any toppings or grains you have on hand.

FOR THE RED SNAPPER

½ pound (225g) red snapper, skin and bones removed, then diced

1 tablespoon (15ml) peanut oil or olive oil

FOR THE DRESSING

¼ cup (60ml) soy sauce

2 tablespoons (30ml) sesame oil

2 tablespoons (30ml) fresh lime juice

1 tablespoon (15ml) fresh lemon juice

1 teaspoon (5ml) sriracha sauce

TO ASSEMBLE

1 cup (237ml) cooked wheat berries

1 cup (237ml) cooked bulgur wheat

2 avocados, peeled, pitted, and diced

¼ red onion, thinly sliced

1 cucumber, diced

1 scallion, thinly sliced

Sesame seeds

For the Red Snapper

Preheat the water bath to 110°F (43.3°C).

Salt and pepper the fish, place in the sous vide bag with the oil, then seal. Let the fish sit for 30 minutes for the dry brine to take effect. Place the bag in the water bath and cook the fish for 15 to 45 minutes, until heated through.

For the Dressing

Whisk all the ingredients together, then salt and pepper to taste.

To Assemble

Take the sous vide bag out of the water and remove the cooked fish from the bag.

Place the wheat berries and bulgur in a bowl. Top with the snapper, avocado, red onion, and cucumber. Drizzle the dressing on top. Sprinkle the scallions and sesame seeds on top, and serve.

MAHI-MAHI GRAIN BOWL

COOKS: 130°F (54.4°C) FOR 15 TO 45 MINUTES | SERVES: 4

Sometimes, when I eat fish as a main course, I end up hungry again in a few hours. Making it the star of a hearty grain bowl ensures I'll be satisfied for hours. You can mix and match the grains—I really like farro and quinoa as well—and you can use any vegetables you want.

This orange vinaigrette is one of my go-to sauces when I want to add a splash of bright flavor to a dish. It comes together quickly and goes with everything from fish to chicken and is even great on a salad.

FOR THE MAHI-MAHI

½ teaspoon (2.5ml) garlic powder

½ teaspoon (2.5ml) ground coriander

¼ teaspoon (1ml) ground cumin

4 mahi-mahi portions, about 6 ounces (170g) each

2 tablespoons (30ml) butter or olive oil

FOR THE ORANGE VINAIGRETTE

3 tablespoons (45ml) fresh orange juice

2 tablespoons (30ml) white wine vinegar

1 tablespoon (15ml) honey

5 tablespoons (75ml) olive oil

1 shallot, diced

TO ASSEMBLE

2 cups (473ml) cooked bulgur

2 cups (473ml) mixed sautéed vegetables (I prefer squash, carrots, broccoli, and bell peppers)

Fresh parsley

For the Mahi-mahi

Preheat the water bath to 130°F (54.4°C).

Mix together the spices in a small bowl. Lightly salt and pepper the fish, then sprinkle with the spices. Place the mahi-mahi in a sous vide bag with the oil and seal. Let the fish sit for 30 minutes for the dry brine to take effect. Place the bag in the water bath and cook the fish for 15 to 45 minutes, until heated through.

For the Orange Vinaigrette

Whisk together the orange juice, vinegar, and honey. Stir in the shallot and let sit for 10 minutes. While whisking, slowly drizzle in the olive oil until fully emulsified and the mixture comes together. Salt and pepper to taste.

To Assemble

Take the sous vide bag out of the water and remove the cooked fish from the bag. Dry it off thoroughly, using paper towels or a clean dish cloth. Lightly salt the fish, then quickly sear one side until it starts to brown. Remove from the heat.

Place the bulgur in a bowl and top with the mahi-mahi, browned side up. Add the sautéed vegetables and parsley, drizzle with the orange vinaigrette, then serve.

SALMON WITH WHITE BEAN PUREE AND GARLIC KALE

COOKS: 130°F (54.4°C) FOR 15 TO 45 MINUTES | SERVES: 4

Salmon is my favorite fish because of its rich flavor and meaty texture. I like to serve it in a variety of ways, but this white bean puree is always a crowd pleaser. The beans are creamy and hearty, with a lot of nuanced flavors. The puree is a great side dish, but I've also used it at parties as a spread for crostini and there is never any left!

FOR THE SALMON

4 salmon portions, about 6 ounces (170g) each

2 tablespoons (30ml) butter or olive oil

FOR THE WHITE BEAN PUREE

1 medium onion, diced

6 cloves garlic, minced

½ teaspoon (2.5ml) smoked paprika

¼ teaspoon (1ml) chipotle pepper powder

2 teaspoons (10ml) dried orange peel

Leaves from 8–10 sprigs fresh thyme

½ cup (118ml) chicken stock

2 cups (473ml) cooked white beans

Juice of ½ lemon

2 tablespoons (30ml) heavy cream

FOR THE GARLIC KALE

1 bunch fresh kale, washed and chopped

5 cloves garlic, minced

1 tablespoon (15ml) minced ginger

1 tablespoon (15ml) sherry vinegar

For the salmon

Preheat the water bath to 130°F (54.4°C).

Salt and pepper the fish and place in the sous vide bag with the butter, then seal. Let the fish sit for 30 minutes for the dry brine to take effect. Place the bag in the water bath and cook the fish for 15 to 45 minutes, until heated through.

For the White Bean Puree

Heat some oil in a pan over medium heat. Add the onions and cook until they have softened, about 4–6 minutes. Add the garlic, paprika, chipotle powder, orange peel, and thyme, then cook until the garlic has softened, about 1 minute. Add the chicken stock and white beans, then bring to a simmer. Cook until the beans are very tender, about 10 minutes. Remove from the heat and let cool.

Once the cooked white bean mixture has cooled, stir in the lemon juice and heavy cream then puree it well. Salt and pepper to taste.

For the Garlic Kale

Heat some oil in a pan over medium heat. Add the kale, garlic, ginger, and vinegar, then cover and let cook until the kale is tender, about 10 to 20 minutes, stirring occasionally and adding small amounts of water as needed.

To Assemble

Take the sous vide bag out of the water and remove the cooked salmon from the bag. Dry it off thoroughly, using paper towels or a clean dish cloth. Lightly salt the fish then quickly sear one side until it starts to brown. Remove from the heat.

To serve, place the white bean puree on a plate, then add the garlic kale next to it. Place the salmon on top, browned side up. Sprinkle with the thyme leaves and sea salt.

> TIP You can replace the chicken stock with 2 more tablespoons (30ml) of cream and ¼ cup (60ml) of water for a vegetarian option.

BOURBON AND BROWN SUGAR–CURED SALMON

COOKS: 110°F (43.3°C) FOR 15 TO 45 MINUTES | SERVES: 4 AS AN APPETIZER

This dish is a cross between cured salmon and sushi. The fish is first lightly cured, infusing it with flavor and contributing a firmness of texture. Once it has been cured, I like to cook it at 110°F (43°C) to give it some structure without drying it out. It's then chilled and thinly sliced, usually as an appetizer, but if you serve it with a salad or steamed vegetables, it would make a delicious light meal.

FOR THE CURED SALMON

½ pound (225g) salmon

Zest of 1 orange

1 tablespoon (15ml) salt

2 tablespoons (30ml) brown sugar

1 tablespoon (15ml) bourbon

TO ASSEMBLE

1 green apple, cored and thinly sliced

1 tablespoon (15ml) chopped fresh dill

For the Cured Salmon

Preheat a water bath to 110°F (43.3°C).

Remove the pin bones and skin from the salmon. Sprinkle the salmon with the orange zest. Combine the salt and brown sugar together in a small bowl, then sprinkle some over the salmon (there may be some left over). Place the salmon in the sous vide bag with the bourbon. Lightly seal the bag and let the fish sit in the refrigerator for at least 30 minutes but preferably several hours for the dry brine to take effect. Place the sous vide bag in the water bath and cook for 15 to 45 minutes, until heated through.

Once cooked, remove the sous vide bag from the water bath and place in an ice bath until chilled.

To Assemble

Take the cooked and chilled salmon out of the sous vide bag and pat dry. Thinly slice the salmon.

Place the sliced green apple on a plate and arrange the salmon around it. Sprinkle with the dill and serve.

SEA BASS WITH FENNEL CARPACCIO

COOKS: 120°F (48.9°C) FOR 15 TO 45 MINUTES | SERVES: 4

This is a bright, citrusy dish that is great as a main course on a warm summer day. The sea bass is lightly poached at 120°F (48.9°C), which gives it a very delicate, buttery texture that complements the crunchy fennel and crispy pickled onions. If you prefer a more traditional texture, you can increase the temperature to 130°F (54.4°C).

The quick pickled onions are a favorite of mine and I also use them on everything from steaks to hot dogs. If you aren't a fan of fennel, or you have trouble finding it, I've also made the carpaccio with kohlrabi, turnips, radishes, and even summer squash. They all contribute a different flavor profile, but each works in its own right.

FOR THE SEA BASS

4 sea bass portions, about 6 ounces (170g) each

2 tablespoons (30ml) butter or olive oil

FOR THE FENNEL CARPACCIO

1 fennel bulb

2 tablespoons (30ml) fresh orange juice

1 tablespoon (15ml) fresh lemon juice

2 tablespoons (30ml) olive oil

FOR THE PICKLED ONIONS

1 red onion, thinly sliced

¼ cup (60ml) red wine vinegar

¼ cup (60ml) water

1 tablespoon (15ml) sugar

TO ASSEMBLE

2 tablespoons (30ml) capers

Zest of 1 orange

Zest of 1 lemon

Zest of 1 lime

Reserved fennel fronds, chopped

Flaky sea salt

For the Sea Bass

Preheat the water bath to 120°F (48.9°C).

Salt and pepper the fish and place in the sous vide bag with the butter, then seal. Let the fish sit for 30 minutes for the dry brine to take effect. Place the bag in the water bath and cook the fish for 15 to 45 minutes, until heated through.

For the Fennel Carpaccio

Remove the root of the fennel. Remove the fronds and reserve them, then thinly slice the fennel.

Add the orange juice, lemon juice, and olive oil in a bowl, then whisk to combine. Add the fennel and toss to coat.

For the Pickled Onions

Place the onion, red wine vinegar, water, and sugar in a pot and bring to a boil. Reduce the heat and let simmer for 5 minutes. Remove from the heat and let cool.

To Assemble

Take the sous vide bag out of the water and remove the cooked fish from the bag. Dry it off thoroughly, using paper towels or a clean dish cloth. Lightly salt the fish, then quickly sear one side until it starts to brown. Remove from the heat.

To serve, place some of the fennel carpaccio on a plate, along with its dressing. Top with a portion of sea bass, browned side up. Add some capers then sprinkle with the citrus zest. Top with some fennel fronds and pickled red onion. Sprinkle with sea salt.

TILAPIA FISH TACOS

COOKS: 130°F (54.4°C) FOR 15 TO 45 MINUTES | SERVES: 4

Fish tacos are great in their own right, but I first started to cook them when my local fish market would sell "chunks" of various fish that were left over from trimming their filets and steaks. The chunks were still the same high-quality fish, they just didn't look "pretty" and were sold at 75 percent off, making fish tacos a cost-effective way to have a tasty dinner. I use tilapia in this recipe, but I've also used salmon, swordfish, and mahi-mahi, so feel free to experiment with whatever fresh fish you can get your hands on.

FOR THE TILAPIA

1 teaspoon (5ml) garlic powder

½ teaspoon (2.5ml) paprika

½ teaspoon (2.5ml) ground cumin

1 pound (450g) tilapia

2 tablespoons (30ml) butter or olive oil

TO ASSEMBLE

8 corn tortillas

1 red bell pepper, roasted and sliced

1 poblano pepper, roasted and sliced

1 cup (237ml) cooked corn kernels

1 onion, sliced and sautéed

1 radish, sliced

1 cup (237ml) watercress

1 lime, cut into eighths

For the Tilapia

Preheat the water bath to 130°F (54.4°C).

Mix together the spices in a small bowl. Lightly salt and pepper the fish, then sprinkle with the spices. Place the fish in a sous vide bag with the butter and seal. Let the fish sit for 30 minutes for the dry brine to take effect. Place the bag in the water bath and cook the fish for 15 to 45 minutes, until heated through.

To Assemble

Take the sous vide bag out of the water and remove the cooked fish from the bag. Dry it off, then flake the fish apart into bite-size pieces.

Place a corn tortilla on each plate, and add about ¼ cup tilapia pieces, then top with some vegetables. Sprinkle with the watercress then squeeze some lime on top and serve.

GREEN APPLE SALAD WITH SOY-CURED TURBOT

COOKS: 110°F (43.3°C) FOR 15 TO 45 MINUTES | SERVES: 4

Turbot has been showing up more and more at fish markets. It is relatively inexpensive and mild-tasting, making it a great candidate for a flavorful cure. This cure, utilizing soy sauce, fish sauce, and miso paste, replaces the usual dry brine I use on fish. It infuses the fish with umami, while also firming up the fish for cooking. If you can't seal liquids, you can let the fish sit in the brine to cure, then pour out the brine before sealing.

FOR THE TURBOT

2 tablespoons (30ml) soy sauce

2 teaspoons (10ml) fish sauce

2 teaspoons (10ml) miso paste

¼ teaspoon (1ml) chipotle pepper powder or cayenne pepper powder

Freshly ground pepper

4 turbot portions, about 6 ounces (170g) each

FOR THE GREEN APPLE SALAD

2 Granny Smith apples

12 green beans

2 cloves garlic, minced

1 serrano pepper, seeded and minced

1 tablespoon (15ml) fish sauce

1 tablespoon (15ml) fresh lime juice

½ cup (118ml) shredded carrots

8 cherry tomatoes, halved

TO ASSEMBLE

Fresh cilantro, chopped

Roasted peanuts, coarsely chopped

For the Turbot

Preheat the water bath to 110°F (43.3°C).

Mix the soy sauce, fish sauce, miso paste, and pepper powder together to form a wet brine. Pepper the turbot then brush liberally with the wet brine. Place in the sous vide bag, then lightly seal. Let the turbot sit for 30 to 60 minutes for the brine to take effect. Then, place the bag in the water bath and cook for 15 to 45 minutes, until heated through.

For the Green Apple Salad

Clean the outside of the apples and remove the cores. Cut them into matchsticks or use a mandolin or spiralizer. Clean the green beans, cut them into 2" (50mm) pieces then cut into quarters lengthwise.

Mix together the garlic, serrano pepper, fish sauce, and lime juice. Toss mixture with the green apple, green beans, and shredded carrots. Salt and pepper to taste, then stir in the cherry tomatoes.

To Assemble

Take the sous vide bag out of the water and remove the cooked fish from the bag. Dry it off thoroughly, using paper towels or a clean dish cloth.

To serve, place some of the green apple salad on a plate and top with the turbot. Garnish with cilantro and roasted peanuts.

 TIP The wet brine makes the fish a bit salty, so I like to pair it with a tart and spicy green apple salad.

LOBSTER TAILS WITH TARRAGON BUTTER

COOKS: 131°F (55°C) FOR 20 TO 40 MINUTES | SERVES: 4

I have cooked lobsters several different ways, from boiling them whole to steaming only the claws, but the most efficient method I have found for a weekday meal is to sous vide the lobster tail itself. Sous vide ensures that it is cooked completely through and it is at the specific temperature you want.

I like to add the butter and tarragon to the sous vide bag so they are infused together, then use the leftover liquid as a dipping sauce for the lobster. I prefer my lobster cooked at 131°F (55°C), but 140°F (60°C) will give you a more traditional texture. For a much softer texture, you can drop the temperature even lower.

FOR THE LOBSTER TAILS

4 lobster tails, shell removed (see Tip)

6 tablespoons (90ml) butter

8 fresh tarragon sprigs

TO ASSEMBLE

1 lemon, cut into eighths

Sea salt

For the Lobster Tails

Preheat a water bath to 131°F (55°C).

Lightly salt and pepper the lobster, place in the sous vide bag with the butter and tarragon sprigs on top of the tails, then seal. Place the bag in the water bath and cook the lobster for 20 to 40 minutes, until heated through.

To Assemble

Take the sous vide bag out of the water and remove the lobster tails. Place one on each plate. Pour the juices from the sous vide bag into ramekins or dipping dishes (this is the tarragon butter). Squeeze some lemon on top of the lobster, sprinkle with the sea salt, and then serve along with the dipping sauce.

> **TIP** To remove the lobster from the shell, you can either cut the shell off with kitchen shears or boil the lobster for 1 to 2 minutes and chill it in an ice bath. Once removed from the ice bath, you can separate the meat from the shell with your hands.

SCALLOPS WITH MANGO SALSA

COOKS: 122°F (50°C) FOR 15 TO 35 MINUTES | SERVES: 4

Since scallops are usually just pan-fried for a few minutes, they tend to be one of those dishes that many people wonder why you should even sous vide. The biggest advantage is ensuring they are cooked all the way through, but the lower temperature also firms up the scallops, giving them a distinctive texture that is hard to achieve through traditional means. I like to pair the scallops with an effortless mango salad that contributes sweetness and spice to the meal without overpowering the delicate flavor of the scallops.

FOR THE SCALLOPS

1 pound (450g) large dry sea scallops

FOR THE MANGO SALSA

2 mangos, peeled and diced

1 shallot, sliced

½ serrano pepper, seeded and diced

1 tablespoon (15ml) fresh lime juice

1 tablespoon (15ml) olive oil

TO ASSEMBLE

Fresh basil leaves, coarsely chopped

For the Scallops

Preheat the water bath to 122°F (50°C).

Salt and pepper the scallops, then place them in the sous vide bag in a single layer. Lightly seal the bag and place it in the water bath to cook for 15 to 35 minutes until heated through.

For the Mango Salsa

Combine all the ingredients in a bowl.

To Assemble

Take the sous vide bag out of the water and remove the cooked scallops from the bag. Dry them off thoroughly, using paper towels or a clean dish cloth. Lightly salt the scallops, then quickly sear one side until it starts to brown. Remove from the heat.

To serve, place some scallops on a plate, browned side up. Add a spoonful of the mango salsa and sprinkle with the chopped basil leaves.

> TIP Make sure you buy dry sea scallops. They have a much better texture and the size is ideal for searing, compared to the blander wet scallops and smaller bay scallops.

SHRIMP AND CHEESE GRITS

COOKS: 130°F (54.4°C) FOR 15 TO 35 MINUTES | SERVES: 4

This is a hearty meal that works for brunch or dinner. Sous vide shrimp always turn out tender, and 130°F (54.4°C) is my favorite temperature for them, though my wife prefers 140°F (60°C). Adding onions, peppers, and mushrooms give this dish its heft.

If you want lighter grits, you can omit the butter and heavy cream. I also like to add a splash of soy sauce and miso paste to the grits for even more umami flavor, but, if you can't find miso paste, you can leave it out.

FOR THE SHRIMP

½ teaspoon (2.5ml) garlic powder

½ teaspoon (2.5ml) onion powder

½ teaspoon (2.5ml) sweet paprika

1 pound (450g) shrimp, peeled and cleaned

1 tablespoon (15ml) olive oil or butter

FOR THE SAUTÉED VEGETABLES

1 yellow onion, diced

1 red bell pepper, diced

1 yellow bell pepper, diced

3 cloves garlic, minced

8 ounces (225g) baby bella mushrooms, coarsely chopped

FOR THE GRITS

1 cup (237ml) grits

1 tablespoon (15ml) soy sauce

1 tablespoon (15ml) miso paste

2 tablespoons (30ml) butter

2 tablespoons (30ml) heavy cream

2 tablespoons (30ml) fresh grated parmesan cheese

⅓ cup (78ml) grated cheddar cheese

TO ASSEMBLE

Fresh parsley, chopped

For the Shrimp

Preheat a water bath to 130°F (54.4°C).

Mix the spices together in a bowl. Sprinkle the spice mixture over the shrimp, then place in a sous vide bag in a single layer. Add the butter, seal the bag, then cook for 15 to 35 minutes, until heated through.

For the Sautéed Vegetables

Heat some olive oil in a pan over medium heat. Add the onions and cook until beginning to soften, about 4–8 minutes. Add the peppers and garlic then cook until softened, about 3 minutes. Remove the vegetables from the pan and set aside.

Add some more olive oil to the pan and add the mushrooms. Cook until lightly browned on all sides, 10 to 20 minutes. Remove from the heat and combine with the onions and peppers.

For the Grits

Prepare the grits according to package directions, with the addition of the soy sauce and miso paste. Once cooked, stir in the butter, cream, and cheeses. Salt and pepper to taste.

To Assemble

Place the grits in a bowl and top with the sautéed vegetables. Remove the shrimp from the sous vide bag and place it on top of the grits. Sprinkle with the parsley and serve.

SHRIMP WITH SUMMER SUCCOTASH

COOKS: 130°F (54.4°C) FOR 15 TO 35 MINUTES | SERVES: 4

I only recently started making succotash, or even knew what it was! As I eat it more, I've discovered that I really enjoy the combination of beans and corn with a little citrus and spice added. It's a great summer dish, but it can also be gratifying in wintertime. Here I top it with sous vided shrimp, but for a more robust meal you can pair it with chicken or even steak.

FOR THE SHRIMP

1 pound (450g) shrimp, peeled and cleaned

2 tablespoons (30ml) butter or olive oil

FOR THE SUCCOTASH

1 red onion, diced

2 cloves garlic, minced

1 poblano pepper, diced

2 cups (473ml) corn kernels

2 cups (473ml) lima beans

2 tablespoons (30ml) butter

Juice of 1 lime

TO ASSEMBLE

1 lime, cut into eighths

2 tablespoons (30ml) chopped fresh basil leaves

For the Shrimp

Preheat the water bath to 130°F (54.4°C).

Place the shrimp in a sous vide bag in a single layer, add the butter, and seal. Place the bag in the water bath and cook the shrimp for 15 to 35 minutes, until heated through.

For the Succotash

Heat some olive oil in a pan over medium-high heat. Place the red onion in the pan and cook until it starts to soften, about 4–8 minutes. Add the garlic and poblano peppers and cook until the poblano peppers are tender, about 3 minutes. Add the corn and lima beans and cook until the lima beans are tender. Add butter and let it melt. Juice the lime into the pan and mix well to combine.

To Assemble

Take the sous vide bag out of the water and remove the cooked shrimp from the bag.

Place a few spoonfuls of succotash on a plate, then top with the shrimp. Add a lime wedge or two, then sprinkle with the fresh basil and serve.

SQUID PUTTANESCA OVER ANGEL HAIR PASTA

COOKS: 138°F (58.9°C) FOR 2 TO 4 HOURS | SERVES: 4

Puttanesca is a hearty sauce that packs a real punch. I pair it with some sous vided squid, which adds extra texture to the dish, and serve it over angel hair pasta. I usually use Kalamata or other high-quality brined olives to maximize the flavor. If you can find them with the pits removed, it will also greatly speed up your prep work.

Squid can become really tough when cooked traditionally, but with sous vide it is much more forgiving. My mother-in-law has been cooking squid her whole life, but once she tried using sous vide she never went back. After it is sous vided, you can also sear the squid if you like, which will firm it up slightly.

FOR THE SQUID

1 teaspoon (5ml) garlic powder

½ teaspoon (2.5ml) fresh thyme leaves

¼ teaspoon (1ml) red pepper flakes

¾ pound (340g) squid, cleaned and cut into rings

FOR THE PUTTANESCA SAUCE

3 tablespoons (45ml) olive oil

5 cloves garlic, minced

4 anchovy fillets, finely minced

½ teaspoon (2.5ml) red pepper flakes

3 tablespoons (45ml) chopped capers

¼ cup (60ml) chopped olives

1½ cups (355ml) crushed tomatoes

¼ cup (60ml) chopped fresh parsley

TO ASSEMBLE

4 portions of cooked angel hair pasta (about 1 pound)

Zest of 1 lemon

¼ cup (60ml) chopped fresh parsley

Red pepper flakes

For the Squid

Preheat a water bath to 138°F (58.9°C).

Mix the spices together in a bowl. Salt and pepper the squid, then sprinkle with some of the spice mixture. Place in the sous vide bag, lightly seal, and place in the water bath. Cook the squid for 2 to 4 hours, until tenderized.

For the Puttanesca Sauce

Place the oil, garlic, anchovies and red pepper flakes in a pan and heat over medium heat. Once the garlic just starts to brown, add the capers, olives, and crushed tomatoes. Bring the mixture to a simmer and let it cook until it thickens to your desired consistency. Remove from the heat and stir in the parsley.

To Assemble

Remove the squid from the sous vide bag. Place a mound of the pasta on a plate and top with a spoonful or two of the puttanesca sauce. Place some squid on top, then sprinkle with the lemon zest, parsley, and red pepper flakes. Drizzle olive oil on the top and serve.

CHAPTER 5

Fruits and Vegetables

FRUITS AND VEGETABLES SOUS VIDE

When it comes to using sous vide, there's one aspect that is often overlooked: sous vide vegetables and fruits. While I do think sous vide has the biggest benefits with meat, it also makes some tasty vegetables that many people swear by!

Almost all vegetables are cooked at 183°F (83.9°C) or higher. This is because most vegetables are held together with pectin, which only begins to break down above 180°F to 183°F (82.2°C to 83.9°C). Hotter temperatures will tenderize the vegetables more quickly, but basically they will have the same texture at the end.

The normal cook times for fruits and vegetables are between 25 and 90 minutes, with the tougher vegetables taking longer. The longer they cook, the more tender they will get. There is a whole lot of variety in fruits and vegetables, so be aware that all cooking times are estimates. For example, a late-season, ripe bosc pear will cook much faster than an early-season, slightly underripe one will.

When bagging your fruits and vegetables, make sure they are in a single layer in the bag to ensure even cooking. I try to keep my bags under 1" (25mm) thick.

Probably the biggest issue when sous viding vegetables is preventing the bags from floating. Most vegetables float and many give off gases as they cook that expand the bag. I've found magnets work well to hold the bags down, as do sous vide weights. I'll also often leave the bag unsealed with the edge out of the water and hanging over the side of the container. This allows the air and gases to escape and helps prevent floating.

ASPARAGUS WITH LEMON-CAPER SAUCE

COOKS: 183°F (83.9°C) FOR 10 TO 30 MINUTES | SERVES: 4 AS A SIDE

Asparagus is a pretty straightforward vegetable to cook, but using sous vide gives you a little more wiggle room on the timing. It works especially well on thicker asparagus, since the lower temperature allows it to cook through without overcooking the outsides. The timing depends on the thickness and tenderness of the asparagus. Thin asparagus can be done in as little as 10 minutes, while thicker ones can take upwards of half an hour.

Asparagus has a distinctive flavor on its own, so I like to use a low-key lemon-caper sauce to brighten it up without overpowering it.

FOR THE ASPARAGUS

2 bunches asparagus, cleaned and ends trimmed

FOR THE LEMON-CAPER SAUCE

6 tablespoons (90ml) butter

2 shallots, sliced

4 cloves garlic, minced

2 tablespoons (30ml) capers

2 tablespoons (30ml) fresh lemon juice

TO ASSEMBLE

3 tablespoons (45ml) chopped fresh parsley

Zest of 1 lemon

For the Asparagus

Preheat the water bath to 183°F (83.9°C).

Salt and pepper the asparagus spears, put in the sous vide bag, then seal. Place the bag in the water bath and cook the asparagus for 10 to 30 minutes, until heated through and tender.

For the Lemon-Caper Sauce

Place the butter in a pot over medium heat and melt. Add the shallots and garlic, and cook them until they soften, about 4–6 minutes. Stir in the capers and lemon juice, then remove from the heat.

To Assemble

Take the sous vide bag out of the water, remove the asparagus from the bag, and place on a plate. Spoon the lemon-caper sauce, including the shallot and garlic pieces, on top of the asparagus. Top with the parsley and lemon zest, then serve.

BEET SALAD WITH GOAT CHEESE

COOKS: 183°F (83.9°C) FOR 60 TO 90 MINUTES | SERVES: 4 AS A SIDE

Beets are a favorite food of my mother-in-law, so I try to make them occasionally to impress her! They work well with sous vide because it can tenderize them without drying them out or turning them into mush.

There are many ways to finish off beets, but I enjoy this salad, which combines the beets with bright oranges and rich goat cheese. It is rounded out with some sweet balsamic vinegar and toasted walnuts.

FOR THE BEETS

8 medium-sized beets

Zest of 1 orange

TO ASSEMBLE

2 tablespoons (30ml) chopped fresh tarragon leaves

Zest of 1 orange

1 shallot, thinly sliced

2 cups (473ml) lightly packed arugula

1 cup (237ml) crumbled goat cheese, preferably chèvre

½ cup (118ml) walnuts

Balsamic vinegar

For the Beets

Preheat the water bath to 183°F (83.9°C).

Peel the beets and cut them into bite-size chunks. Zest the orange over the beets, then salt and pepper them. Place the beets in a sous vide bag, trying to keep the thickness of the bag less than 1" (25mm) for even cooking. Seal the bag, then place in the water bath and cook for 60 to 90 minutes, until heated through and tender.

To Assemble

Take the sous vide bag out of the water bath and remove the beets. Toss the beets with the tarragon, orange zest, shallots, and arugula, and place in a serving bowl. Top with some goat cheese and walnuts, then drizzle with the balsamic vinegar and serve.

> **TIP** Beets stain, so be sure to cover your cutting board with parchment paper or plastic wrap. I also wear plastic gloves to keep my hands from turning red.

LEMON-PARMESAN BROCCOLI

COOKS: 183°F (83.9°C) FOR 30 TO 60 MINUTES | SERVES: 4 AS A SIDE

I usually like broccoli prepared in one of two ways—either smothered in melted cheese and bacon, or served simply by itself. While I prefer the melted-cheese version, my waistline makes a good argument that a little parmesan cheese and lemon juice would be the better option for me. You can also toss in cauliflower, green beans, or parsnips to add some variety to the dish.

FOR THE BROCCOLI

1 head of broccoli

¼ teaspoon (1ml) red pepper flakes

TO ASSEMBLE

½ cup (118ml) freshly grated parmesan cheese

1 lemon

For the Broccoli

Preheat a water bath to 183°F (83.9°C).

Cut the broccoli into florets and place in the sous vide bag with the pepper flakes. Salt and pepper the broccoli, then seal the bag, trying to keep the thickness of the bag less than 1" (25mm) for even cooking. Place the bag in the water bath and cook for 30 to 60 minutes, until tender.

To Assemble

Take the sous vide bag out of the water, remove the broccoli, and place into serving bowls. Sprinkle the parmesan cheese on top of the broccoli. Squeeze the lemon over the top and serve.

MAPLE-MISO–GLAZED BUTTERNUT SQUASH

COOKS: 183°F (83.9°C) FOR 30 TO 60 MINUTES | SERVES: 4 AS A SIDE

The combination of miso and maple syrup was introduced to me by my friend Sean when I visited him in North Carolina. He used it as a glaze for sliced acorn squash and it was amazing. I've started to use this version on butternut squash, mainly because it is easier to peel and cube, but you can use any winter squash you like. Once the squash has become tender, it is briefly cooked to reduce the juices and then mixed with maple syrup and lemon juice.

FOR THE BUTTERNUT SQUASH

2 cups (473ml) peeled, coarsely chopped butternut squash

1 tablespoon (15ml) butter or olive oil

1 teaspoon (5ml) miso paste

1 teaspoon (5ml) sweet paprika

TO ASSEMBLE

2 tablespoons (30ml) maple syrup

1 lemon

For the Butternut Squash

Preheat the water bath to 183°F (83.9°C).

Combine all ingredients in a bowl and toss to mix well. Salt and pepper the squash, then pour into a sous vide bag, trying to keep the thickness of the bag less than 1" (25mm) for even cooking. Seal the bag and place it in the water bath. Cook for 30 to 60 minutes, until tender.

To Assemble

Take the sous vide bag out of the water, pour the butternut squash and its juices into a pan, and heat over medium-high heat until the juices have started to thicken. Drizzle with the maple syrup and zest the lemon on top. Squeeze some lemon juice, about ¼ of a lemon, on top and taste for balance. Cook until the sauce has thickened to desired consistency. Remove from the heat and serve.

HONEY-CHIPOTLE–GLAZED CARROTS

COOKS: 183°F (83.9°C) FOR 45 TO 60 MINUTES | SERVES: 4 AS A SIDE

I eat a lot of carrots, and this combination of honey and chipotle is one of my favorite ways to prepare them. The sous vide process tenderizes them, while still leaving some bite, and the glazing process at the end coats them with the sweet and spicy sauce. Feel free to increase or decrease the amount of chipotle peppers, or even omit them entirely, to match the spiciness you prefer.

FOR THE RAINBOW CARROTS

8–12 carrots, peeled and cut into 3" (76mm) sticks

2 tablespoons (30ml) butter

1 teaspoon (5ml) diced chipotles in adobo sauce

TO ASSEMBLE

Zest and juice of 1 lemon

Honey

Coarse sea salt

For the Rainbow Carrots

Preheat the water bath to 183°F (83.9°C).

Combine all ingredients into a sous vide bag, then salt and pepper them. Trying to keep the thickness of the bag less than 1" (25mm) for even cooking, seal the bag. Place the bag in the water bath and cook for 45 to 60 minutes, until tender.

To Assemble

Zest the lemon and reserve the zest.

Take the sous vide bag out of the water, pour the carrots and their juice into a pan, and heat over medium-high heat. Drizzle with the honey and squeeze some lemon juice, about ¼ of the lemon, on top and taste for balance. Cook until the sauce has just thickened, then remove from the heat. Plate the carrots with the sauce, sprinkle with the sea salt, and serve.

BUFFALO-STYLE CAULIFLOWER

COOKS: 183°F (83.9°C) FOR 20 TO 30 MINUTES | SERVES: 4 AS A SIDE

I've been cooking more and more cauliflower lately, mainly because my father-in-law loves it, but also because so many people discount it. It actually has a lot of versatility and with its mild taste it easily picks up flavors from sauces. In this recipe I like to turn it into a spicy Buffalo-style cauliflower with blue cheese. It helps me get my Buffalo wing fix without having to go to the bar!

The Buffalo sauce should lightly coat the cauliflower, but if you want it to be stronger, just make some extra sauce and spoon it over the cauliflower after the sous vide process is done.

FOR THE CAULIFLOWER

- 1 head of cauliflower, cut into florets
- 4 tablespoons (60ml) hot sauce (such as Frank's RedHot®)
- 2 tablespoons (30ml) butter
- 2 teaspoons (10ml) Worcestershire sauce

TO ASSEMBLE

- 2 tablespoons (30ml) blue cheese crumbles
- 1 tablespoon (15ml) finely chopped parsley

For the Cauliflower

Preheat a water bath to 183°F (83.9°C).

Place all the ingredients in a sous vide bag, then salt and pepper them. Trying to keep the thickness of the bag less than 1" (25mm) for even cooking, seal the bag. Place the bag into the water bath and cook for 20 to 30 minutes, until tender.

To Assemble

Remove the cauliflower from the sous vide bag and top with the crumbled blue cheese and parsley, and serve.

POACHED CHERRY TOMATOES

COOKS: 131°F (55°C) FOR 30 MINUTES | SERVES: 4 AS A SIDE

A quick way to add a flavorful side dish to your meal is to lightly poach tomatoes using sous vide. I usually serve them with steaks, so I cook them at 131°F (55°C). I toss them in with the steaks at the end of their cooking time, and the same process would work well for pork or chicken; just reduce the time slightly. I add olive oil as well as fresh rosemary and thyme to create some depth of flavor, but the dish is almost completely free of active cooking time.

FOR THE POACHED TOMATOES

2 pints (950ml) cherry tomatoes

4 tablespoons (60ml) good olive oil

1 tablespoon (15ml) chopped fresh rosemary leaves

1 teaspoon (5ml) fresh thyme leaves

For the Poached Tomatoes

Preheat a water bath to 131°F (55°C).

Put the cherry tomatoes, olive oil, rosemary, and thyme in a sous vide bag. Mix together well, then salt and pepper the tomatoes. Trying to keep the thickness of the bag less than 1" (25mm) for even cooking, lightly seal the bag. Place the bag in the water bath and cook the tomatoes for 30 minutes, until heated through.

To Assemble

Take the sous vide bag out of the water and remove the cooked tomatoes. Place in a bowl and serve as a side.

SWEET CORN WITH CURRIED-LIME BUTTER

COOKS: 183°F (83.9°C) FOR 15 TO 25 MINUTES | SERVES: 4 AS A SIDE

I think fresh sweet corn right off the farm is one of the joys of summer. I'll often enjoy it cooked on the grill, but sometimes I want something more hands-off and I'll end up sous viding it for a more tender version. There are many ways to finish off corn, but I like this curried-lime butter as a way to add a lot of flavor to the dish. You can increase or decrease the amount of curry paste to better suit your own spice preferences.

Corn can vary widely in its tenderness, so it's often best to eat a kernel raw before cooking it. This will give you an idea of how sweet and tender it already is and can help determine cooking time.

FOR THE CORN

4 ears of corn

2 tablespoons (30ml) butter

FOR THE CURRIED-LIME BUTTER

½ cup (118ml) unsalted butter, softened at room temperature

Zest of 1 lime

1 teaspoon (5ml) fresh lime juice

1 teaspoon (5ml) honey

1 teaspoon (5ml) red curry paste

TO ASSEMBLE

Fresh cilantro, finely chopped

For the Corn

Preheat the water bath to 183°F (83.9°C).

Remove the husks from the corn and discard. Salt and pepper the corn, then place the ears of corn into the sous vide bag in a single layer with the butter. Seal the bag, then place it in the water bath to cook them for 15 to 25 minutes, until tender.

For the Curried-Lime Butter

Place all the ingredients into a bowl and mix together thoroughly.

To Assemble

Take the sous vide bag out of the water bath and remove the cooked corn. Salt and pepper the corn, then smear with the curried-lime butter. Top with the fresh cilantro and serve.

RUSTIC MASHED RED POTATOES

COOKS: 183°F (83.9°C) FOR 30 TO 60 MINUTES | SERVES: 4 AS A SIDE

Mashed potatoes are one of my favorite foods There are many ways to cook the potatoes, but sous vide is an easy, hands-off choice. This recipe is for straightforward mashed potatoes with just a few herbs for flavor, but you can add in roasted garlic, horseradish, or other herbs and spices. I prefer a more rustic mashed potato, but for a smoother style you can whip the potatoes with a wooden spoon or run them through a ricer or tamis.

FOR THE POTATOES

2 pounds (900g) red potatoes, coarsely diced

1 teaspoon (5ml) fresh thyme leaves

2 tablespoons (30ml) butter

TO ASSEMBLE

5 tablespoons (75ml) butter

⅔ cup (158ml) whole milk or heavy cream

3 tablespoons (45ml) chopped fresh basil

2 tablespoons (30ml) chopped fresh parsley

For the Potatoes

Preheat the water bath to 183°F (83.9°C).

Place the potatoes in a sous vide bag, then salt and pepper them, and add the thyme and butter. Trying to keep the thickness of the bag less than 1" (25mm) for even cooking, seal the bag. Place the bag in the water bath and cook for 30 to 60 minutes, until tender.

To Assemble

Remove the potatoes from the bag and place in a large bowl. Add the butter, milk, basil, and parsley, and mash with a potato masher or a large fork. Do not overmash or the potatoes will take on a tacky texture. Salt and pepper to taste and serve.

WARM POTATO SALAD WITH MUSTARD VINAIGRETTE

COOKS: 183°F (83.9°C) FOR 30 TO 60 MINUTES | SERVES: 4 TO 6 AS A SIDE

Many traditional potato salads are mayonnaise-based and served cold, but this one has a mustard and vinegar backbone and is served hot. It really complements fattier main dishes, like rib eye or pork shoulder, because the vinegar and mustard will cut the richness. While it's a great barbecue side, especially because it can sit out in the sun without going bad, it also doesn't look out of place on a holiday table next to a prime rib or ham.

FOR THE POTATOES

2 pounds (900g) potatoes, coarsely diced

2 teaspoons (10ml) fresh rosemary leaves

FOR THE SAUTÉED VEGETABLES

4 strips of cooked bacon

2 carrots, peeled and diced

2 cloves garlic, diced

3 shallots, diced

FOR THE DRESSING

3 tablespoons (45ml) olive oil

2 tablespoons (30ml) apple cider vinegar

2 tablespoons (30ml) Dijon mustard

TO ASSEMBLE

1 tablespoon (15ml) chopped fresh parsley

1 tablespoon (15ml) chopped fresh dill

2 teaspoons (10ml) chopped chives

For the Potatoes

Preheat the water bath to 183°F (83.9°C).

Place the potatoes in a sous vide bag, then salt and pepper them, and add the rosemary. Trying to keep the thickness of the bag less than 1" (25mm) for even cooking, seal the bag. Place the bag in the water bath and cook for 30 to 60 minutes, until tender.

For the Sautéed Vegetables

In a pan over medium-low heat sauté the bacon until it begins to crisp and the fat is rendered, about 10–15 minutes. Remove half the bacon fat from the pan. Add the carrots, garlic, and shallots to the pan, and cook until the garlic and shallots become soft, about 5 minutes.

For the Dressing

Whisk together the olive oil, vinegar, and mustard.

To Assemble

Take the sous vide bag out of the water bath, remove the cooked potatoes, and place them in a large bowl. Pour the sautéed vegetable mixture on top and add the dressing. Stir everything together until it is mixed well. Sprinkle the parsley, dill, and chives on top and serve.

SPICED SWEET POTATOES WITH MAPLE DRIZZLE

COOKS: 183°F (83.9°C) FOR 45 TO 60 MINUTES | SERVES: 4 AS A SIDE

Sweet potatoes are good in so many different preparations and this recipe doubles down on the sweetness factor. The potatoes are diced and then sous vided with butter and spices until tender. They are then topped with sweet maple syrup, roasted pecans, and fresh thyme leaves. The sweet potatoes are a flavorful, sweet, and lightly savory side dish that complements rich meats.

FOR THE SWEET POTATOES

⅛ teaspoon (0.5ml) ground nutmeg

⅛ teaspoon (0.5ml) ground cloves

⅛ teaspoon (0.5ml) ground cinnamon

2 pounds (900g) sweet potatoes, coarsely diced

2 tablespoons (30ml) butter

TO ASSEMBLE

Maple syrup

3 tablespoons (45ml) chopped roasted pecans

½ teaspoon (2.5ml) fresh thyme leaves

For the Sweet Potatoes

Preheat the water bath to 183°F (83.9°C).

Mix together the spices in a small bowl. Place the sweet potatoes in a sous vide bag, then salt and pepper them. Add the butter and sprinkle with the spices, then seal, trying to keep the thickness of the bag less than 1" (25mm) for even cooking. Place the bag in the water bath and cook for 45 to 60 minutes, until tender.

To Assemble

Remove the sweet potatoes from the sous vide bag and place them in a serving bowl. Drizzle with the maple syrup, sprinkle with the pecans and thyme leaves, then serve.

BUTTER-POACHED TURNIPS

COOKS: 183°F (83.9°C) FOR 45 TO 60 MINUTES | SERVES: 4 AS A SIDE

I was never a big fan of turnips until I grew my own. Then I realized just how much more flavor they have than the ones from the grocery store. This is a simple recipe, with just some herbs, cumin, and lemon to complement the turnips, so I highly recommend picking up some from a local farmers' market to maximize their taste. This recipe also works well with carrots, parsnips, and other root vegetables.

FOR THE TURNIPS

3 cups (710ml) coarsely chopped turnips

2 tablespoons (30ml) butter

2 sprigs fresh thyme

½ teaspoon (2.5ml) ground cumin

TO ASSEMBLE

Zest of 1 lemon

Fresh oregano leaves

Coarse sea salt

For the Turnips

Preheat the water bath to 183°F (83.9°C).

Combine all ingredients in a sous vide bag, then salt and pepper them. Trying to keep the thickness of the bag less than 1" (25mm) for even cooking, seal the bag. Place the bag in the water bath and cook for 45 to 60 minutes, until tender.

To Assemble

Take the sous vide bag out of the water and remove the cooked turnips from the bag. Place the turnips on a plate. Zest the lemon on top, then add the oregano leaves. Sprinkle with the sea salt, then serve.

DILLY BEANS

COOKS: 183°F (83.9°C) FOR 30 TO 45 MINUTES | MAKES: 1 PINT (473ML) OF PICKLES

Dilly beans are pickled green beans and are usually flavored with dill and garlic. They are quick to put together and work as a great topping for beef or pork, or on their own as a snack.

Many sous vide pickling recipes use lower temperatures to preserve the crispness of the vegetables, but this one uses a higher temperature to soften up the beans, and it also works well with carrots, cucumbers, or other tougher vegetables. The timing varies based on the vegetable, but I usually cook them less time, so they maintain a little crunch. You can also mix up the spices and herbs to create your own flavor profiles.

FOR THE BRINE

½ cup (118ml) water

½ cup (118ml) white wine vinegar

2 tablespoons (30ml) sugar, optional

½ tablespoon (7.5ml) salt

FOR THE PICKLES

1 pint (473ml) green beans, cleaned

4 sprigs fresh dill

2 cloves garlic, coarsely chopped

½ teaspoon (2.5ml) black peppercorns

½ teaspoon (2.5ml) whole cumin seeds

½ teaspoon (2.5ml) red pepper flakes

For the Brine

Combine all the ingredients in a bowl and whisk until the sugar and salt dissolve.

For the Pickles

Preheat the water bath to 183°F (83.9°C).

Place the green beans, dill, and garlic in a pint (473ml) Mason jar, leaving some room at the top. Add the peppercorns, cumin seeds, and red pepper flakes. Fill the jar with enough brine to cover the vegetables while still leaving some headspace at the top. Screw the lid on the jar until it's finger-tight, basically until you feel medium resistance when tightening using only your fingertips. This will allow some air to escape during the sous vide process and help prevent breakage. Place the jar in the water bath and cook for 30 to 45 minutes, or until crisp-tender.

Once the pickles are cooked, remove the jar from the water bath and let them cool on the counter or in a room-temperature water bath. Place the jar of pickled beans in the refrigerator and use as desired.

BROWN SUGAR–BOURBON APPLES

COOKS: 185°F (85°C) FOR 90 TO 120 MINUTES | SERVES: 4 AS A SIDE

These sweet and spicy apples are a versatile dish that can be used as a side or a dessert. They go great with fatty or smoked meats, like brisket, pulled pork, or prime rib. They make a savory topping for ice cream or brownies as well. You can also leave out the thyme and chipotle pepper powder for a sweeter, less savory take.

FOR THE APPLES

2 Braeburn or other baking apples, cored and cut into thick slices

2 tablespoons (30ml) brown sugar

1 tablespoon (15ml) maple syrup

½ teaspoon (2.5ml) fresh thyme leaves

2 teaspoons (10ml) fresh lemon juice

1 tablespoon (15ml) melted butter

⅛ teaspoon (0.5ml) chipotle pepper powder

TO ASSEMBLE

3 tablespoons (45ml) bourbon

Maple syrup

2 teaspoons (10ml) chopped fresh mint leaves

For the Apples

Preheat the water bath to 185°F (85°C).

Toss the apples and other ingredients together, then place in a sous vide bag, trying to keep the thickness of the bag less than 1" (25mm) for even cooking. Seal the bag and place it in the water bath. Cook for 90 to 120 minutes, until tender.

To Assemble

Take the sous vide bag out of the water, remove the cooked apples, and place in a bowl. Pour the juices from the bag into a pot, along with the bourbon, and bring to a simmer, being careful to prevent flare-ups from the bourbon. Cook until it has thickened slightly, then pour over the apples. Drizzle the apples with the maple syrup, then sprinkle with the mint leaves and serve.

WARM PEACH AND ALMOND SALAD

COOKS: 165°F (73.9°C) FOR 20 TO 40 MINUTES | SERVES: 4 AS A SIDE

This is a straightforward side dish or snack that lets the flavor of the peaches shine. They are cooked long enough to take on a tender, firm texture. The bourbon and cinnamon infuse the peaches with their flavors, while the almonds provide a nice crunch. This salad works best in the height of peach season, though sometimes I eat them all before I get around to actually cooking them!

FOR THE PEACHES

4 peaches, pits removed and cut in half

¼ teaspoon (1ml) ground cinnamon

1 tablespoon (15ml) bourbon

TO ASSEMBLE

¼ cup (60ml) chopped almonds

Molasses

8 fresh mint leaves, coarsely chopped

For the Peaches

Preheat a water bath to 165°F (73.9°C).

Sprinkle the peaches with the cinnamon. Place in a sous vide bag with the bourbon, then lightly seal. Place the bag in the water bath and cook the peaches for 20 to 40 minutes, until heated through and tender.

To Assemble

Take the sous vide bag out of the water, then remove the peaches from the bag and place them on a plate. Pour some of the juices over the peaches. Top with the almonds, then drizzle with the molasses. Top with the mint and serve.

CHAPTER 6

Grains, Custards, and Sauces

GRAINS, CUSTARDS, AND SAUCES SOUS VIDE

The majority of foods sous vided are meat, fish, and vegetables, but there are actually a lot of other uses for water baths. In this chapter I share some recipes that make cooking grains, and creating tender custards and unbroken sauces a snap. These recipes take advantage of sous vide's ability to hold food at a set temperature. This capability can be used to easily prepare items that need to be held at constant temperatures, such as yogurt, cheese, custards, and some egg preparations, like lemon curd.

Most of these types of dishes are cooked in Mason jars or ramekins. When using ramekins, the level of the water is always lower than the lip of the container. If you need to use deeper water, you can often place the ramekins on a wire rack to keep them out of the water. Mason jars can be placed directly in the water with the lid finger tightened so bubbles can escape if the buildup of pressure becomes too great.

But don't limit yourself to the usual. Because of the constantly held temperatures, some people have used sous vide to temper chocolate, decrystalize honey, steep expensive tea, brew beer, as a circulated bath for keeping beer and wine cold, to develop film, and even as a foot soaking bath!

SIMPLE SOUS VIDE GRAINS

COOKS: 183°F (83.9°C) FOR 20 TO 60 MINUTES | MAKES: 1 PINT (473ML)

Most grains are convenient to cook with sous vide, not only because it makes it easy to replicate your results, but also because there is no cleanup. I usually use 1-pint (473ml) or 1-quart (950ml) Mason jars to cook the grains, depending on how much I need. You can also mix and match grains, as long as they get done at about the same time.

The cooking time will depend entirely on the type of grain, but, in general, it takes about 20 percent longer than is called for on the stovetop. The amount of liquid needed is also dependent on the grain, but is generally about 80 percent of what you usually need due to the lack of evaporation. I have used the recipe below on quinoa, farro, bulgur wheat, and several other grains with great success.

FOR THE SOUS VIDE GRAINS
⅔ cup (158ml) grains
1⅓ cups (315ml) water
Dash of salt

For the Sous Vide Grains

Preheat a water bath to 183°F (83.9°C).

Combine the grains, water, and salt in a pint (473ml) jar, leaving a little headspace at the top. Screw the lid on the jar until it's finger-tight, basically until you feel medium resistance when tightening using only your fingertips. This will allow some air to escape during the sous vide process and help prevent breakage. Shake the jar, then carefully place it in the water bath. Cook the grains for 20 to 60 minutes, until the water is absorbed and the grains are cooked through. Remove from the jar and fluff with a fork before serving.

APPLE-CINNAMON OATMEAL

COOKS: 183°F (83.8°C) FOR 30 TO 45 MINUTES | MAKES: 1 PINT (473ML)

Oatmeal is one of those dishes that isn't too hard to cook traditionally, but I use sous vide a lot for the convenience. I eat oatmeal almost every morning, and I like to make a large pot ahead of time. Since you can cook and store the oatmeal in the same Mason jar, there is no cleanup of a pot and spoon, making it quick and easy to do. This recipe incorporates apples and cinnamon, adding crisp bursts of sweetness and sharp background notes.

FOR THE OATMEAL

⅔ cup (158ml) Bob's Red Mill Organic Quick Cook Steel Cut Oats

¼ cup (60ml) diced apple

1⅓ cups (315ml) water

¼ teaspoon (1ml) ground cinnamon

Dash of salt

TO ASSEMBLE

Maple syrup

Almond slivers

Thinly sliced apple

For the Oatmeal

Preheat a water bath to 183°F (83.8°C).

Combine the oats, apple, water, cinnamon, and salt in a pint (473ml) jar. Screw the lid on the jar until it's finger-tight, basically until you feel medium resistance when tightening using only your fingertips. This will allow some air to escape during the sous vide process and help prevent breakage.

Shake the jar, then carefully place it in the water bath. Cook the oatmeal for 30 to 45 minutes, until the water is absorbed and the oatmeal is cooked through, shaking the jar once or twice during the process.

To Assemble

Spoon the oatmeal into a bowl. Drizzle with maple syrup, then top with almond slivers and apple slices.

TIP For this recipe I use Bob's Red Mill® Organic Quick Cook Steel Cut oats, but you can use any oatmeal you'd like. Just change the time and water amounts. In general, it takes about 20 percent longer than is called for on the stovetop, and the amount of liquid needed is only about 80 percent of what you usually need, due to the lack of evaporation.

HOMEMADE YOGURT WITH BERRIES

COOKS: 110°F (43.3°C) FOR 5 HOURS | MAKES: 4 CUPS YOGURT

To make yogurt, you heat milk or cream to above 180°F (82.2°C), cool it down, mix in a starter culture, then let it incubate at 100°F (37.8°C) to 120°F (48.9°C) for several hours. Using a sous vide machine allows you to easily maintain the temperatures you are looking for during the yogurt-making process.

Sous vide yogurt is typically made in glass jars with the lids either off or not fully tightened. The starter bacteria will give off gases as they create the yogurt, so a sealed container may leak or explode. The yogurt is usually made in the container you will store or serve it from because moving it to a new one can affect its consistency. You can use the sous vide machine to reach both temperatures, but I typically just heat the milk on the stove because it's much quicker than raising and lowering the temperature of the whole water bath.

FOR THE YOGURT

4 cups (946ml) half and half or milk

½ cup (118ml) plain yogurt with live and active cultures

TO ASSEMBLE

Mixed berries

Granola mix

Honey

For the Yogurt

Fill a water bath to about an inch (25mm) below the height of the jars you are using and preheat the water to 110°F (43.3°C).

Heat the half and half in a pot on the stove to at least 180°F (82.2°C). Remove it from the heat and let it cool to at least 120°F (48.9°C). Then whisk in the yogurt with the live and active cultures. Pour the mixture into the Mason jars and seal each one with plastic wrap. Place the jars into the water bath and let incubate for 5 hours.

After 5 hours, remove the jars from the water bath and refrigerate until chilled. Once the yogurt is cold, seal with the Mason jar lids. It will last in the refrigerator for 1 to 2 weeks.

To Assemble

Place some berries in a bowl and cover with a spoonful or two of the yogurt. Top with some granola mix and drizzle some honey on top.

> **TIP** I use half and half, which results in a very thick yogurt. If you prefer a thinner one, you can substitute whole or 2 percent milk. To get the incubation going, you need to add ½ cup (118ml) of yogurt that contains live and active cultures. Yogurt that contains this type of culture will be labeled on the package. The length of the incubation time adds tanginess to the yogurt and can range from 3 to 24 hours.

CRÈME FRAICHE

COOKS: 95°F (35°C) FOR 8 TO 10 HOURS | MAKES: 1 PINT (473ML)

Crème fraiche is a "soured cream" that is often served as a topping on fresh fruit or pies. In addition, it is an excellent way to enrich soups and pan sauces. This crème fraiche may not be as sour as typical American sour cream but still has a delicate tangy flavor.

Crème fraiche is made with cream and a culture, usually derived from buttermilk or yogurt, that is incubated at room temperature over 24 hours. Using sous vide to culture the crème fraiche speeds up the process to only 8 to 10 hours and maintains complete control over the temperature.

FOR THE CRÈME FRAICHE

- 2 cups (473ml) heavy cream or whipping cream, not ultra-pasteurized
- 3 tablespoons (45ml) cultured buttermilk

For the Crème Fraiche

Fill a water bath to about an inch (25mm) below the height of the Mason jars you are using and preheat the water to 95°F (35°C).

Whisk together the heavy cream and buttermilk. Pour the mixture into a canning jar and screw the lid on the jar until it's finger-tight, basically until you feel medium resistance when tightening using only your fingertips. This will allow some air to escape during the sous vide process and help prevent breakage. Place the jar into the water bath and let cook for 8 to 10 hours.

Remove the jar from the water bath, chill in an ice bath, and refrigerate. It will last for 1 to 2 weeks in the refrigerator.

> TIP Be sure you do not use ultra-pasteurized cream. It doesn't work nearly as well as raw or regular pasteurized cream does.

CLASSIC CRÈME BRÛLÉE

COOKS: 190°F (87.8°C) FOR 60 TO 90 MINUTES | MAKES: 4 CRÈME BRÛLÉES

Most people think crème brûlée is a fancy dish, but it's actually very straightforward and simple to make. Using a sous vide machine makes it even easier. This is a classic crème brûlée, and you can take it in a variety of directions, depending on the flavors you want.

The best depth for the crème brûlée is usually less than an inch (25mm) deep; otherwise, the inside might not cook all the way through. For deeper crème brûlées, you may need to increase the cooking time to offset the depth. If your ramekins are touching each other in the water bath, it can help to rotate them halfway through the cooking process to ensure they cook evenly.

FOR THE CRÈME BRÛLÉE

2 cups (473ml) heavy or whipping cream
1 vanilla bean
1 cinnamon stick
4 egg yolks
Pinch of salt
⅓ cup (78ml) sugar

TO ASSEMBLE

Sugar
Fresh mint leaves

> **TIP** To get the ramekins at the proper height, it is helpful to put a bowl or strainer upside down in the water bath and place a plate or sheet pan on top of it where the ramekins can sit. Be sure to maintain the water level throughout the cooking process.

For the Crème Brûlée

Place an upside-down strainer or bowl in your water bath. Top with a baking sheet or plate. Set the ramekins on the baking sheet and fill the water bath two-thirds of the way up the ramekins. Preheat the water bath to 190°F (87.8°C).

Pour the heavy cream into a pot. Split the vanilla bean and scrape out the seeds, then add the seeds and the bean to the cream. Add the cinnamon stick. Bring just to a simmer, stirring frequently. Turn off the heat and let it infuse for 10 minutes. Strain the cream.

Whisk together the egg yolks in another bowl, then slowly whisk in the salt and sugar. The mixture should turn glossy and thicken slightly. Slowly whisk in the infused cream.

Evenly divide the mixture among the ramekins, cover each ramekin with plastic wrap, and use a rubber band to hold it in place. Place the ramekins in the sous vide bath with the water level coming two-thirds of the way up the side. Cook for 60 to 90 minutes, depending on how thick you prefer your crème brûlée.

Once cooked, remove the ramekins from the water bath and let the crème brûlée cool for 15 to 20 minutes. Place in the refrigerator and chill until firm, or preferably overnight.

To Assemble

Spread a thin layer of sugar a few grains thick on the top of each crème brûlée and quickly torch until the sugar melts and begins to brown. Add a few mint leaves and serve.

DULCE DE LECHE

COOKS: 185°F (85°C) FOR 10 TO 15 HOURS | MAKES: 1 PINT (473ML)

Dulce de leche is a caramel-like sauce made from sweetened condensed milk that is excellent drizzled on berries or baked desserts, like brownies or cake. It's very easy to make at home, especially using a sous vide machine. At its most basic, you place a can of sweetened condensed milk in a water bath set to 185°F (85°C) and cook it for 10 to 15 hours. But for best results I like to add a little vanilla paste and salt. I make it in ½-pint (237ml) Mason jars because of their great size and their even cooking.

FOR THE DULCE DE LECHE

2 (14-ounce [400g]) cans sweetened condensed milk

½ teaspoon (2.5ml) vanilla paste or extract

1 teaspoon (5ml) salt

For the Dulce de Leche

Preheat a water bath to 185°F (85°C).

Whisk together the sweetened condensed milk, vanilla paste, and salt, then pour into 4 ½-pint (237ml) jars. Screw the lid on the jars until they're finger-tight, basically until you feel medium resistance when tightening using only your fingertips. This will allow some air to escape during the sous vide process and help prevent breakage.

Place into the water bath and let cook for 10 to 15 hours, until the milk has browned and thickened.

Remove the jars from the water bath, let cool, then refrigerate. The dulce de leche will last for several months in the refrigerator.

BÉARNAISE SAUCE

COOKS: 149°F (65°C) FOR 30 MINUTES | MAKES: 1 CUP (237ML)

A béarnaise sauce is very similar to a hollandaise sauce, but white wine and vinegar add the acidity in béarnaise and it is flavored with shallots and tarragon. It is usually used as a sauce for steak or other grilled meat. This is another sauce that tends to break apart when made traditionally, but with sous vide it stays together much better and the results are more consistent.

FOR THE BÉARNAISE SAUCE

½ cup (118ml) dry white wine

¼ cup (60ml) champagne vinegar or white wine vinegar

1 shallot, minced

2 tablespoons (30ml) chopped fresh tarragon leaves

3 egg yolks

8 tablespoons (118ml) unsalted butter, cut into cubes or melted

For the Béarnaise Sauce

Preheat the water bath to 149°F (65°C).

Combine the wine, vinegar, shallots, and 1 tablespoon (15ml) of the tarragon in a small pot, and bring to a simmer. Reduce until most of the liquid has evaporated and about 2 tablespoons (30ml) remain, about 5–15 minutes. Strain out the liquid, pressing on the shallots to remove it all, and reserve. Discard the solids.

Combine the liquid with the egg yolks and butter in a Ziploc bag or a pint (473ml) Mason jar and seal. Place in the water bath and cook for 30 minutes.

Remove from the heat and pour into a blender. Blend until smooth. Add the remaining tarragon, then season with salt and pepper.

HOLLANDAISE SAUCE

COOKS: 149°F (65°C) FOR 30 MINUTES | MAKES: 1 PINT (473ML)

Hollandaise sauce is an egg-and-butter–based sauce that is rich, delicate, and full of flavor. There are a few different ways to prepare it, but a large issue is trying to prevent the sauce from "breaking" and separating into its component parts. Using sous vide is by far the easiest method to use mainly because it is the least prone to breaking. All you need to do is combine the ingredients in a Ziploc bag or pint (473ml) Mason jar, cook it at around 149°F (65°C) for about 30 minutes, then blend it together.

I love using hollandaise sauce on eggs benedict, as well as salmon or asparagus.

FOR THE HOLLANDAISE SAUCE

3 egg yolks

8 tablespoons (118ml) unsalted butter

1 tablespoon (15ml) fresh lemon juice

Pinch of cayenne pepper powder

For the Hollandaise Sauce

Preheat the water bath to 149°F (65°C).

Combine all the ingredients in a Ziploc bag or pint (473ml) Mason jar and seal. Place in the water bath and cook for 30 minutes.

Remove from the heat and pour into a blender. Blend until smooth, then season with salt and pepper.

ORANGE CURD

COOKS: 165°F (73.9°C) FOR 45 TO 60 MINUTES | MAKES: 1 PINT (473ML)

Orange curd is a sweet and sour, jamlike condiment that is great on pastries and tarts and can even be worked into savory dishes. Using sous vide to make it takes much of the guesswork out of the process and makes it a very hands-off dish. This recipe makes a thick curd. For a thinner one, just reduce the gelatin by about 50 percent.

FOR THE ORANGE CURD

3 large eggs, slightly beaten

½ cup (118ml) sugar

⅓ cup (78ml) fresh squeezed orange juice

Zest of 3 oranges

4 tablespoons (60ml) butter, melted

1 teaspoon (5ml) unflavored gelatin

For the Orange Curd

Preheat a water bath to 165°F (73.9°C).

Place all the ingredients into a sous vide bag and mix together well. Seal the bag and place it in the water bath. Cook for 45 to 60 minutes.

Once cooked, remove the bag from the water bath, pour the orange mixture into a blender, and process until fully emulsified. Let cool, or chill in an ice bath, and then pour into a container to set and refrigerate until ready to use. It will last 1 to 2 weeks in the refrigerator. For a puddinglike consistency, you can blend the set curds.

CHAPTER 7

Infusions

INFUSIONS WITH SOUS VIDE

Using sous vide to make infusions was something that took me a while to get into, but once I did, I started to do it all the time! There are a lot of uses for infusions, from making flavored vinegars and oils to alcohols, syrups, and specialty cocktails.

Most traditional infusions require days or weeks, but with sous vide this time can be reduced to a few hours. You also have complete control over the infusion temperature, which allows you to instill different flavors into your infusions. Something infused at 130°F (54.4°C) will taste slightly different than the same ingredients infused at 185°F (85°C).

The sous vide infusion process is fairly straightforward. Combine a liquid you want to infuse, such as alcohol, vinegar, oil, or water, with some flavoring agents, like herbs, spices, or fruits. I generally combine them in a canning jar, but sous vide bags work just as well.

Place the infusion in a water bath, usually set to between 131°F (55°C) and 176°F (80°C). Let the infusion cook for about 1 to 3 hours, or up to 12 hours for some oil infusions.

Once cooked, remove the infusion from the water bath and chill it completely. Strain the infusion and it is ready to use.

Don't hesitate to experiment with different ingredients that sound good to you. Many of the sous vide infusions are practically foolproof, and I'm sure you'll love the results!

TIP If you find yourself making a lot of infusions, I highly recommend purchasing an apparatus known as a canning jar lifter. It only costs a few dollars and makes the process of moving hot Mason jars around so much easier than other methods.

MEYER LEMON OLIVE OIL

COOKS: 140°F (60°C) FOR 4 TO 5 HOURS | MAKES: 1½ CUPS (355ML)

Good friends of ours have a Meyer lemon tree in their yard, and it inspired me to create this recipe. Using Meyer lemons results in a slightly sweeter flavor, but you can make this oil with regular lemons if that is all you can find. I like to incorporate this infused olive oil as part of a vinaigrette for an herb salad or to drizzle over grilled fish. The olive oil contributes a mellow pungency, but if you want a purer lemon taste, you can use a neutral oil like grapeseed or canola.

FOR THE MEYER LEMON OLIVE OIL

3–4 Meyer lemons

1½ cups (355ml) olive oil

For the Meyer Lemon Olive Oil

Preheat a water bath to 140°F (60°C).

Lightly scrub the outside of the lemons, then remove the zest with a vegetable peeler or zester. Make sure little to no pith came off in the process, using a paring knife to remove any.

Combine the lemon peels and olive oil in a sous vide bag or a pint (473ml) Mason jar. Seal the lid and place in the water bath. Heat the infusion for 4 to 5 hours.

Prepare an ice bath with half ice and half water. Remove the bag or jar from the water bath and place in the ice bath for 15 to 20 minutes. Strain the infusion, discard the solids, and store in a sealed container.

LIMONCELLO

COOKS: 140°F (60°C) FOR 1 TO 3 HOURS | MAKES: 3 CUPS (710ML)

Limoncello was the first infused alcohol I ever made, and it is still one of my favorites. I recently brought some to my Italian mother-in-law and even she approved of it! The recipe involves infusing vodka with lemon peel and then mixing it with simple syrup. I recommend starting by adding only half the simple syrup and tasting it; that way you can make it as sweet or as strong as you want. This recipe also works well with limes, oranges, and other citrus for fun variations on the drink. Using the infused lemon vodka in a martini or mixed drink is also a great way to go!

FOR THE LEMON VODKA

5 lemons

1½ cups (355ml) vodka

FOR THE SIMPLE SYRUP

1 cup (237ml) water

1 cup (237ml) sugar

For the Lemon Vodka

Preheat a water bath to 140°F (60°C).

Lightly scrub the outside of the lemons and remove the zest with a vegetable peeler or zester. Make sure little to no pith came off in the process, using a paring knife to remove any.

Place the peels and vodka in a sous vide bag or canning jar, then seal and place in the water bath. Heat the infusion for 1 to 3 hours.

Prepare an ice bath with half ice and half water. Remove the bag or jar from the water bath and place in the ice bath for 15 to 20 minutes. Strain the vodka infusion, discarding the solids.

For the Simple Syrup

Combine the water and sugar in a pot and heat over medium-high heat, stirring occasionally until the sugar has completely dissolved. Remove from the heat and let cool. The simple syrup can be stored in the refrigerator for several weeks.

To Assemble

Stir or blend the lemon vodka and simple syrup together and, ideally, let the mixture sit overnight in the refrigerator for the flavors to meld. It is now ready to use or can be stored in the refrigerator for several weeks.

CHERRY-VANILLA RUM

COOKS: 140°F (60°C) FOR 1 TO 2 HOURS | MAKES: 1½ CUPS (355ML)

Here the sweet and tart cherry flavors go wonderfully with the earthy vanilla. This recipe also works well with any light alcohol, like vodka or silver tequila, and I've used it successfully with bourbon. It is even great to make infused vinegars.

Once you've infused the rum, you can use it in a lot of ways. I especially like it in daiquiris or mojitos, and if you add some simple syrup it is terrific with club soda over ice for a refreshing fizz.

You can also save the cherries you used to infuse the rum. They will be very boozy with vanilla undertones and make a fabulous cocktail garnish or dessert topping. To sweeten them up, store them in simple syrup.

FOR THE CHERRY-VANILLA RUM

15 cherries, pitted and stemmed

1 vanilla bean, split lengthwise

1½ cups (355ml) white or silver rum

For the Cherry-Vanilla Rum

Preheat a water bath to 140°F (60°C).

Place the cherries in a sous vide bag or canning jar. Lightly crush or muddle the cherries. Add the vanilla bean, pour the rum on top, then seal and place in the water bath. Heat the infusion for 1 to 2 hours.

Prepare an ice bath with half ice and half water. Remove the bag or jar from the water bath and place in the ice bath for 15 to 20 minutes. Strain the infusion. It is now ready to use or can be stored in in a sealed container in the refrigerator for several months.

 TIP Cherries stain, so be sure to cover your cutting board with parchment paper or plastic wrap.

BASIL AND ROSEMARY OLIVE OIL

COOKS: 140°F (60°C) FOR 4 TO 5 HOURS | MAKES: 1½ CUPS (355ML)

Infusing traditional Italian herbs and red pepper flakes into olive oil results in an aromatic oil that is great when drizzled on fish, vegetables, or poultry. This also makes an amazing dipping oil for fresh bread. You can make a variation of this oil with any herbs you have on hand; each one will contribute its own unique flavor profile, but the end result is always tasty.

FOR THE BASIL AND ROSEMARY OIL

15 fresh basil leaves

3 sprigs fresh rosemary

½ teaspoon (2.5ml) red pepper flakes

1½ cups (355ml) olive oil

For the Basil and Rosemary Oil

Preheat a water bath to 140°F (60°C).

Combine all ingredients in a sous vide bag or a pint (473ml) Mason jar, then seal and place in the water bath. Heat the infusion for 4 to 5 hours.

Prepare an ice bath with half ice and half water. Remove the bag or jar from the water bath and place in the ice bath for 15 to 20 minutes. Strain the infusion, discard the solids. It is now ready to use or can be stored in in a sealed container for several weeks.

GINGER SIMPLE SYRUP

COOKS: 165°F (73.9°C) FOR 2 TO 4 HOURS | MAKES: 2 CUPS (473ML)

This ginger syrup is an excellent way to easily add the spiciness of ginger to cocktails. It can also be combined with club soda to make ginger ale or naturally fermented into ginger beer for refreshing summer drinks. Making your own ginger syrup allows you to control the spiciness, depending on your final planned use of it. This recipe also works well with other flavorful ingredients, such as cinnamon and cloves, mint, or the components in root beer.

FOR THE GINGER SIMPLE SYRUP

1 cup (237ml) sugar

1 cup (237ml) water

5" (125mm) knob fresh ginger, thinly sliced

For the Ginger Simple Syrup

Preheat a water bath to 165°F (73.9°C).

Combine all ingredients in a sous vide bag or a pint (473ml) Mason jar, then seal and place in the water bath. Heat the infusion for 2 to 4 hours, shaking vigorously twice during the infusion process to evenly distribute the sugar.

Prepare an ice bath with half ice and half water. Remove the bag or Mason jar from the water bath and place in the ice bath for 15 to 20 minutes. Strain the infusion and discard the solids. It is now ready to use or can be stored in in a sealed container in the refrigerator for one week.

STRAWBERRY-RHUBARB VINEGAR

COOKS: 140°F (60°C) FOR 1 TO 3 HOURS | MAKES: 1½ CUPS (355ML)

Two of my favorite spring flavors are strawberry and rhubarb. Unfortunately, both of them are in season only for a short time, so I try to preserve them for use all year round. Infusing white wine vinegar with strawberry and rhubarb is a fantastic way to have it on hand throughout the year.

You can use this vinegar as part of a vinaigrette or to brighten up a sauce, but I think it really shines when mixed with some simple syrup and club soda for a refreshing spring shrub.

FOR THE STRAWBERRY-RHUBARB VINEGAR

1½ cups (355ml) coarsely chopped rhubarb stalks (remove all leaves)

1 cup (237ml) coarsely chopped strawberries

2 fresh mint sprigs

1½ cups (355ml) white wine vinegar

For the Strawberry-Rhubarb Vinegar

Preheat a water bath to 140°F (60°C).

Combine all ingredients in a sous vide bag or a pint (473ml) Mason jar, then seal and place in the water bath. Heat the infusion for 1 to 3 hours.

Prepare an ice bath with half ice and half water. Remove the bag or jar from the water bath and place in the ice bath for 15 to 20 minutes. Strain the infusion, discard the solids. It is now ready to use or can be stored in in a sealed container for several months.

BLACKBERRY-BASIL VINEGAR

COOKS: 140°F (60°C) FOR 1 TO 3 HOURS | MAKES: 1½ CUPS (355ML)

Blackberries and basil may seem like a strange combination, but I stumbled across it a few years ago and I keep coming back to it. Infusing them into vinegar preserves their flavor. As an added bonus, they turn the vinegar a beautiful purple that is striking when used tableside. I like to drizzle this over fish or turn it into a shrub with the addition of some simple syrup and club soda.

FOR THE BLACKBERRY-BASIL VINEGAR

½ lime

1½ cups (355ml) blackberries

1 bunch fresh basil, about 10 sprigs

1½ cups (355ml) white wine vinegar

For the Blackberry-Basil Vinegar

Preheat a water bath to 140°F (60°C).

Lightly scrub the outside of the lime, then remove the zest with a vegetable peeler or zester. Make sure little to no pith came off in the process, using a paring knife to remove any.

Combine the lime peel with the blackberries and basil in a sous vide bag or a pint (473ml) Mason jar. Lightly muddle the blackberries, then add the vinegar. Seal and place in the water bath. Heat the infusion for 1 to 3 hours.

Prepare an ice bath with half ice and half water. Remove the bag or pint jar from the water bath and place in the ice bath for 15 to 20 minutes. Strain the infusion, and discard the solids. It is now ready to use or can be stored in in a sealed container for several months.

CHILI PEPPER FIRE VINEGAR

COOKS: 140°F (60.0°C) FOR 1 TO 2 HOURS | MAKES: 1½ CUPS (355 ML)

Many hot sauces are chili peppers blended with vinegar and spices. For this recipe I make a super-spicy hot sauce where all the flavor is infused into the vinegar itself. This makes it a great way to selectively add drops of heat to a meal. I recommend wearing gloves when preparing this vinegar; the oil and juices released from the chopping of the chili peppers will stick to your skin for hours and can burn. If you are a real chili head, feel free to increase the amount of chili peppers used.

FOR THE FIRE VINEGAR INFUSION

1 habanero pepper

1 serrano pepper

1 chipotle pepper in adobo sauce

1 poblano pepper

1½ cups apple cider vinegar

For the Fire Vinegar Infusion

Preheat a water bath to 140°F (60.0°C).

While wearing gloves, remove the stems from the chili peppers and coarsely chop the flesh. Combine the peppers, their seeds, and the vinegar in a sous vide bag or Mason jar, then seal and place in the water bath. Heat the infusion for 1 to 2 hours.

Prepare an ice bath with ½ ice and ½ water. Remove the bag or Mason jar from the water bath and place in the ice bath for 15 to 20 minutes. Strain the vinegar and store in a sealed container.

Cooking Times and Temperatures

There are two ways to cook sous vide; one is based on the thickness of the food and the other is based on the desired tenderness. When cooking is based on the thickness of the food, it is helpful to have a reference guide to fall back on. I've combined several of the respectable sous vide charts into one easy-to-use reference. Both methods have their uses. Thickness-based is ideal for very tender cuts cooked by people who need them done in the minimum amount of time. Tenderness-based is best for tougher cuts or people that have a range of time that they are interested in. This section focuses on thickness and the next is on tenderness.

Cooking by Thickness

Cooking sous vide based on thickness basically tells you the minimum time you can cook a piece of meat to ensure it is safe and comes up to temperature in the middle. It doesn't take in to account tenderizing time or any other factors.

Cooking based on thickness is how PolyScience, Baldwin, and Nathan started out as they did research on food safety. Cooking by thickness is most often used by restaurants or home cooks who want to minimize cooking time and are using tender cuts of meat that don't need any tenderization.

NOTES ON THE THICKNESS TIMES

The times were extrapolated from the descriptions in Baldwin's Practical Guide to Sous Vide as well as Nathan's tables on eGullet and a few other sources.

The times given are approximate since there are many factors that go in to how quickly food is heated. For example, the density of the food matters, which is one reason beef heats differently than chicken. To a lesser degree where you get your beef from will also affect the cooking time, and whether the beef was factory raised, farm raised, or grass-fed. Because of this, I normally don't try to pull the food out at the exact minute it is done unless I'm in a real rush.

The times shown are also the minimum times to heat or pasteurize the food. The food can be, and sometimes needs to be, left in for longer periods in order to fully tenderize the meat. If you are cooking food longer, remember that food should not be cooked at temperatures less than 131°F (55°C) for more than 4 hours.

For a printable version of these charts you can download the ruler from my website at:

AFMEasy.com/HRuler.

Thickness Times for Beef, Lamb, and Pork

These are the times for heating, cooling, and pasteurizing beef, lamb, and other red meat, as well as pork. These times apply to most types of meat except fish, though chicken and poultry are almost always cooked to pasteurization and have been moved to their own section for clarity. If you have some other type of meat (moose, bear, rabbit, etc.) you can use these charts as well.

HEATING TIMES FOR BEEF, LAMB, AND PORK

These times specify how long it takes a piece of meat, with a particular shape, to heat all the way to the center. The center of the meat will come up to about 1° less than the water bath temperature in the time given. The final degree takes a much longer time and generally does not contribute to the final taste or texture.

While there are slight differences in the heating time for different temperatures of water baths, the times usually vary less than 5 to 10 percent even going from a 111°F bath to a 141°F bath (43.8°C to 60.5°C), which equates to a difference of 5 minutes every hour. I show the largest value in the chart.

Remember that you should not cook food at much less than 130°F (54.5°C) for more than 4 hours. If you want to cook a piece of food at a lower temperature, you can cut it into smaller portions so it heats more quickly. The times shown are also minimum times and food can be, and sometimes needs to be, left in for longer periods in order to fully tenderize it.

STARTING TEMPERATURE:	FRIDGE	FRIDGE	FREEZER	FREEZER
SHAPE OF MEAT:	SLAB	CYLINDER	SLAB	CYLINDER
2.75" (70mm)	—	3:30	—	5:00
2.50" (63mm)	5:10	2:50	—	4:20
2.25" (57mm)	4:25	2:20	6:35	3:45
2.00" (51mm)	3:35	2:00	5:30	3:00
1.75" (44mm)	3:00	1:30	4:30	2:30
1.50" (38mm)	2:20	1:10	3:20	1:50
1.25" (32mm)	1:40	0:55	2:35	1:20
1.00" (25mm)	1:15	0:40	1:50	1:00
0.75" (19mm)	0:50	0:30	1:15	0:45
0.50" (13mm)	0:30	0:15	0:40	0:25
0.25" (6mm)	0:10	0:06	0:15	0:15

PASTEURIZATION TIMES FOR BEEF, LAMB, AND PORK

If you want to ensure that your food is safe to eat through pasteurization, then you can follow these sous vide times. They let you know how long you need to cook something, specifically most red meat, for it to be effectively pasteurized and safe to eat.

Like the heating and cooling times, they are not exact, but they are also on the longer side for safety reasons.

THICKNESS	131°F (55°C)	135°F (57°C)	140°F (60°C)
2.75" (70mm)	6:30	5:15	4:00
2.50" (63mm)	5:40	4:35	3:35
2.25" (57mm)	5:10	4:00	3:05
2.00" (51mm)	4:30	3:20	2:30
1.75" (44mm)	4:00	3:00	2:15
1.50" (38mm)	3:25	2:25	1:55
1.25" (32mm)	3:10	2:05	1:40
1.00" (25mm)	2:45	2:00	1:30
0.75" (19mm)	2:30	1:45	1:15
0.50" (13mm)	2:10	1:25	0:50
0.25" (6mm)	1:50	1:00	0:35

COOLING TIMES FOR BEEF, LAMB, AND PORK

If you are cooking food and then storing it in the refrigerator or freezer, then these sous vide cooling times will give you the time that food needs to be in an ice bath before the center is chilled out of the danger zone.

Just like with heating, the actual temperature change isn't a big factor in the time needed to cool it. Just make sure the ice bath is at least one half ice to ensure proper cooling.

STARTING TEMP:	HOT	HOT
SHAPE OF MEAT:	CYLINDER	SLAB
2.75" (70mm)	2:45	5:30
2.50" (63mm)	2:10	4:35
2.25" (57mm)	1:50	4:00
2.00" (51mm)	1:30	3:15
1.75" (44mm)	1:15	2:45
1.50" (38mm)	1:00	2:05
1.25" (32mm)	0:45	1:35
1.00" (25mm)	0:30	1:15
0.75" (19mm	0:20	0:50
0.50" (13mm)	0:15	0:30
0.25" (6mm)	0:10	0:15

Thickness Times for Chicken and Poultry

Sous vide chicken is almost always cooked until it is pasteurized. For heating and cooling times, you can reference the previous section.

PASTEURIZATION TIMES FOR CHICKEN

The sous vide pasteurization times in the chart will ensure that the chicken is always safe to eat. These times are for chicken that has been in the refrigerator; for frozen chicken add some extra time.

THICKNESS	137°F (58°C)	140°F (60°C)	145°F (63°C)	149°F (65°C)
2.75" (70mm)	6:00	5:00	4:15	3:45
2.50" (63mm)	5:20	4:25	3:35	3:10
2.25" (57mm)	4:50	4:05	3:10	2:55
2.00" (51mm)	4:15	3:20	2:30	2:20
1.75" (44mm)	3:45	3:00	2:15	2:00
1.50" (38mm)	3:10	2:30	1:55	1:40
1.25" (32mm)	2:55	2:10	1:40	1:25
1.00" (25mm)	2:15	1:35	1:15	0:55
0.75" (19mm)	2:00	1:20	0:50	0:40
0.50" (13mm)	1:50	1:10	0:35	0:25
0.25" (6mm)	1:40	0:50	0:25	0:20

Heating Times for Fatty Fish

These sous vide times will help you determine how long you need to cook fatty fish in order for it to be brought up to temperature. It will not pasteurize the fish, so make sure you use high-quality fish you would be comfortable eating raw.

There are slight differences in the heating time for different temperatures of water baths, but they usually vary less than 5 to 10 percent even going from a 111°F bath to a 141°F bath (43.8°C to 60.5°C), which equates to a difference of 5 minutes every hour. I show the largest value in the chart.

The chart assumes the fish is defrosted.

THICKNESS	TIME
2.75" (70mm)	3:50
2.50" (63mm)	3:05
2.25" (57mm)	2:40
2.00" (51mm)	2:00
1.75" (44mm)	1:40
1.50" (38mm)	1:20
1.25" (32mm)	0:55
1.00" (25mm)	0:35
0.75" (19mm)	0:21
0.50" (13mm)	0:10
0.25" (6mm)	0:05

Cooking by Tenderness

Cooking by tenderness is dependent on how tender or tough the cut of meat is. Some cuts just need to be heated through, while others need extended cooks of several days until they are broken down enough to enjoy.

To come up with the tenderness times, I've leaned on my own experience and the reports of other people. It is important to understand that all times are estimates, as there are many factors that go in to how tough a piece of meat is. I have cooked a chuck roast for 18 hours and had it turn out too tender, and I've cooked one for 36 hours that was still tough.

The best way to get consistent results is to turn to a butcher or fish monger that you frequent so you can understand how their meat cooks.

The times given are my personal preferences and will get you in the ball park of what you are looking for. If you discover you like something cooked longer or shorter, please go with what you prefer.

Note: For more information about the ranges given, please read my in-depth blog post *Why the Range? Sous Vide Times Explained* AFMEasy.com/HRange.

BEEF, PORK, LAMB, AND OTHER MEAT

Most of the cuts below can have a few different options including "Steak-Like," "TenderSteak," and up to three braising entries.

STEAK-LIKE

Following the "Steak-Like" entry will result in a final dish that has the texture and doneness of a great steak. I recommend starting with 125°F (51.6°C) for rare, 131°F (55°C) for medium rare and 140°F (60°C) for medium. You can then adjust the temperature up or down in future cooks to better match your preference.

General Doneness Range
Rare: 120°F to 129°F (49°C to 53.8°C)
Medium Rare: 130°F to 139°F (54.4°C to 59.4°C)
Medium: 140°F to 145°F (60°C to 62.8°C)
Well Done: Above 145°F (62.8°C)

For the timing, you usually will be given a specific range that I've found to work well for that cut, such as "2 to 4 hours," or "1 to 2 days."

Other timing options are "Time by Thickness" or "Pasteurize by Thickness," which indicates that this cut doesn't need tenderization; it only needs to be heated through and/or pasteurized. You can follow the charts in the Cooking by Thickness section for the specific times. I've used "Pasteurize by Thickness" for entries that are almost always pasteurized, but many people also pasteurize the majority of their meat to be on the safe side.

Warning: If you drop the temperature much below 130°F (54.4°C) you are in the danger zone, not killing any pathogens, and shouldn't cook the food for more than an hour or two.

TENDER STEAK

In addition to the "Steak-Like" entry, some cuts will have a "Tender Steak" entry. These are cuts that are traditionally eaten grilled or pan fried, such as flank, sirloin, or flat iron steaks, but that can also benefit from some tenderization. If you follow the "Steak-Like" entry, they will turn out very similar to the traditionally cooked version, while following the "Tender Steak" entry will result in a much more tender version of that steak.

BRAISE-LIKE

Some cuts can also be traditionally braised, so I give my three favorite time and temperature combinations for them as well.

Most braise-like temperatures range from around 150°F up to 185°F (65.6°C up to 85°C). The temperatures I recommend trying first are:

- 156°F (68.8°C) for a shreddable, but still firm texture
- 165°F (73.9°C) for a more fall-apart texture
- 176°F (80.0°C) for a really fall apart texture

From a timing standpoint, going from 131°F to 156°F (55°C to 68.8°C) seems to cut the cook time in half. Going above 176°F (80.0°C) seems to cut it in half again.

Beef Times and Temperatures

BLADE

Steak-Like: Time by Thickness
Tender Steak: Up to 10 hours

BOTTOM ROUND

Steak-Like: For 2 to 3 days
Braise-Like:
　156°F (68.8°C) for 1 to 2 days
　165°F (73.9°C) for 1 to 2 days
　176°F (80.0°C) for 12 to 24 hours

BRISKET

Steak-Like: For 2 to 3 days
Braise-Like:
　156°F (68.8°C) for 1 to 2 days
　165°F (73.9°C) for 1 to 2 days
　176°F (80.0°C) for 12 to 24 hours

CHEEK

Steak-Like: For 2 to 3 days
Braise-Like:
　156°F (68.8°C) for 1 to 2 days
　165°F (73.9°C) for 1 to 2 days
　176°F (80.0°C) for 12 to 24 hours

CHUCK

Pot Roast
Steak-Like: For 36 to 60 hours
Braise-Like:
　156°F (68.8°C) for 18 to 24 hours
　165°F (73.9°C) for 18 to 24 hours
　176°F (80.0°C) for 12 to 18 hours

EYE ROUND

Steak-Like: For 1 to 2 days
Braise-Like:
　156°F (68.8°C) for 18 to 36 hours
　165°F (73.9°C) for 18 to 36 hours
　176°F (80.0°C) for 8 to 18 hours

FLANK

Bavette
　Steak-Like: Time by Thickness
　Tender Steak: Up to 2 days, I prefer 12 hours

FLAT IRON

Steak-Like: Time by Thickness
Tender Steak: Up to 24 hours

HAMBURGER

Steak-Like: Pasteurize by Thickness

HANGER

Steak-Like: Time by Thickness

LONDON BROIL

Not a true cut but normally flank, chuck, or round
Steak-Like: For 18 to 60 hours
Braise-Like:
　156°F (68.8°C) for 12 to 24 hours
　165°F (73.9°C) for 12 to 24 hours
　176°F (80.0°C) for 8 to 18 hours

PORTERHOUSE

Steak-Like: Time by Thickness

POT ROAST

Steak-Like: For 2 to 3 days
Braise-Like:
　156°F (68.8°C) for 1 to 2 days
　165°F (73.9°C) for 1 to 2 days
　176°F (80.0°C) for 12 to 24 hours

PRIME RIB

Standing Rib Roast, Rib Roast
Steak-Like: Time by Thickness
Tender Steak: Up to 10 hours

RIBEYE

Rib Steak, Delmonico Steak, Scotch Filet, Entrecôte
Steak-Like: Time by Thickness
Tender Steak: Up to 8 hour

RIBS

Beef Spareribs
Steak-Like: For 1 to 2 days
Braise-Like:
    156°F (68.8°C) for 18 to 36 hours
    165°F (73.9°C) for 18 to 36 hours
    176°F (80.0°C) for 8 to 18 hours

SAUSAGE

Steak-Like: Pasteurize by Thickness

SHANK

Shin
Steak-Like: For 2 to 3 days
Braise-Like:
    156°F (68.8°C) for 1 to 2 days
    165°F (73.9°C) for 1 to 2 days
    176°F (80.0°C) for 12 to 24 hours

SHORT RIBS

Back Ribs, Flanken Ribs
Steak-Like: For 2 to 3 days
Braise-Like:
    156°F (68.8°C) for 1 to 2 days
    165°F (73.9°C) for 1 to 2 days
    176°F (80.0°C) for 12 to 24 hours

SHOULDER

Steak-Like: Time by Thickness
Tender Steak: Up to 24 hours

SIRLOIN

Steak-Like: Time by Thickness
Tender Steak: Up to 10 hours

SKIRT

Steak-Like: Time by Thickness
Tender Steak: Up to 24 hours

STEW MEAT

Various Cuts
Steak-Like: For 36 to 60 hours
Braise-Like:
    156°F (68.8°C) for 18 to 24 hours
    165°F (73.9°C) for 18 to 24 hours
    176°F (80.0°C) for 12 to 18 hours

STRIP

Top Loin Strip, New York Strip, Kansas City Strip, Top Sirloin, Top Loin, Shell Steak
Steak-Like: Time by Thickness

SWEETBREADS

Steak-Like: Time by Thickness

T-BONE

Steak-Like: Time by Thickness

TENDERLOIN

Filet mignon, Châteaubriand, Tournedo
Steak-Like: Time by Thickness

TONGUE

Steak-Like: For 2 to 3 days
Braise-Like:
    156°F (68.8°C) for 1 to 2 days
    165°F (73.9°C) for 1 to 2 days
    176°F (80.0°C) for 12 to 24 hours

TOP ROUND

Steak-Like: For 1 to 2 days
Not recommended above 145°F (62.8°C)

TRI-TIP

Steak-Like: Time by Thickness
Tender Steak: Up to 24 hours

Lamb Times and Temperatures

ARM CHOP
Steak-Like: For 18 to 36 hours

BLADE CHOP
Steak-Like: For 18 to 36 hours

BREAST
Steak-Like: For 1 to 2 days
Braise-Like:
  156°F (68.8°C) for 18 to 24 hours
  165°F (73.9°C) for 18 to 24 hours
  176°F (80.0°C) for 12 to 18 hours

LEG, BONE IN
Steak-Like: Time by Thickness
Tender Steak: Up to 24 hours

LEG, BONELESS
Steak-Like: Time by Thickness
Tender Steak: Up to 24 hours

LOIN CHOPS
Steak-Like: Time by Thickness

LOIN ROAST
Steak-Like: Time by Thickness

LOIN, BONELESS
Steak-Like: Time by Thickness

NECK
Steak-Like: For 2 to 3 days
Braise-Like:
  156°F (68.8°C) for 1 to 2 days
  165°F (73.9°C) for 1 to 2 days
  176°F (80.0°C) for 12 to 24 hours

OSSO BUCO
Steak-Like: For 1 to 2 days
Braise-Like:
  156°F (68.8°C) for 18 to 24 hours
  165°F (73.9°C) for 18 to 24 hours
  176°F (80.0°C) for 12 to 18 hours

RACK
Steak-Like: Time by Thickness

RIB CHOP
Steak-Like: Time by Thickness

RIBS
Steak-Like: For 1 to 2 days
Braise-Like:
  156°F (68.8°C) for 18 to 24 hours
  165°F (73.9°C) for 18 to 24 hours
  176°F (80.0°C) for 12 to 18 hours

SHANK
Steak-Like: For 1 to 2 days
Braise-Like:
  156°F (68.8°C) for 18 to 24 hours
  165°F (73.9°C) for 18 to 24 hours
  176°F (80.0°C) for 12 to 18 hours

SHOULDER
Steak-Like: For 1 to 2 days
Braise-Like:
  156°F (68.8°C) for 18 to 24 hours
  165°F (73.9°C) for 18 to 24 hours
  176°F (80.0°C) for 12 to 18 hours

TENDERLOIN
Steak-Like: Time by Thickness

Pork Times and Temperatures

I have replaced "Steak-Like" with "Chop-Like" so it is more accurate but please refer to the "Beef and Red Meat" intro for a full description. My recommended temperatures for "Chop-Like" pork is 135°F (57.2°C), 140°F (60°C), or 145°F (62.8°C), with 140°F (60°C) being my favorite.

ARM STEAK
Chop-Like: For 1 to 2 days

BABY BACK RIBS
Chop-Like: For 1 to 2 days
Braise-Like:
    156°F (68.8°C) for 18 to 24 hours
    165°F (73.9°C) for 18 to 24 hours
    176°F (80.0°C) for 12 to 18 hours

BACK RIBS
Chop-Like: For 1 to 2 days
Braise-Like:
    156°F (68.8°C) for 18 to 24 hours
    165°F (73.9°C) for 18 to 24 hours
    176°F (80.0°C) for 12 to 18 hours

BELLY
Chop-Like: For 2 to 3 days
Braise-Like:
    156°F (68.8°C) for 1 to 2 days
    165°F (73.9°C) for 1 to 2 days
    176°F (80.0°C) for 12 to 24 hours

BLADE CHOPS
Chop-Like: For 8 to 12 hours

BLADE ROAST
Chop-Like: For 1 to 2 days
Braise-Like:
    156°F (68.8°C) for 18 to 24 hours
    165°F (73.9°C) for 18 to 24 hours
    176°F (80.0°C) for 12 to 18 hours

BLADE STEAK
Chop-Like: For 18 to 36 hours

BOSTON BUTT
Chop-Like: For 1 to 2 days
Braise-Like:
    156°F (68.8°C) for 18 to 24 hours
    165°F (73.9°C) for 18 to 24 hours
    176°F (80.0°C) for 12 to 18 hours

BUTT ROAST
Chop-Like: For 1 to 2 days
Braise-Like:
    156°F (68.8°C) for 18 to 24 hours
    165°F (73.9°C) for 18 to 24 hours
    176°F (80.0°C) for 12 to 18 hours

COUNTRY-STYLE RIBS
Chop-Like: For 18 to 36 hours
Braise-Like:
    156°F (68.8°C) for 9 to 18 hours
    165°F (73.9°C) for 6 to 14 hours
    176°F (80.0°C) for 4 to 9 hours

FRESH SIDE PORK
Chop-Like: For 2 to 3 days
Braise-Like:
    156°F (68.8°C) for 1 to 2 days
    165°F (73.9°C) for 1 to 2 days
    176°F (80.0°C) for 12 to 24 hours

GROUND PORK
Pasteurize by Thickness

HAM ROAST

Chop-Like: For 10 to 20 hours

HAM STEAK

Chop-Like: Time by Thickness

LEG (FRESH HAM)

Chop-Like: For 10 to 20 hours

LOIN CHOP

Chop-Like: Pasteurize by Thickness

LOIN ROAST

Chop-Like: Pasteurize by Thickness

PICNIC ROAST

Chop-Like: For 1 to 2 days
Braise-Like:
    156°F (68.8°C) for 18 to 24 hours
    165°F (73.9°C) for 18 to 24 hours
    176°F (80.0°C) for 12 to 18 hours

PORK CHOPS

Chop-Like: Pasteurize by Thickness

RIB CHOPS

Chop-Like: For 5 to 8 hours

RIB ROAST

Chop-Like: For 5 to 8 hours

SAUSAGE

Pasteurize by Thickness

SHANK

Chop-Like: For 1 to 2 days
Braise-Like:
    156°F (68.8°C) for 18 to 24 hours
    165°F (73.9°C) for 18 to 24 hours
    176°F (80.0°C) for 12 to 18 hours

SHOULDER

Chop-Like: For 1 to 2 days
Braise-Like:
    156°F (68.8°C) for 18 to 24 hours
    165°F (73.9°C) for 18 to 24 hours
    176°F (80.0°C) for 12 to 18 hours

SIRLOIN CHOPS

Chop-Like: For 6 to 12 hours

SIRLOIN ROAST

Chop-Like: For 6 to 12 hours

SPARE RIBS

Chop-Like: For 1 to 2 days
Braise-Like:
    156°F (68.8°C) for 18 to 24 hours
    165°F (73.9°C) for 18 to 24 hours
    176°F (80.0°C) for 12 to 18 hours

SPLEEN

Chop-Like: Pasteurize by Thickness

TENDERLOIN

Chop-Like: Pasteurize by Thickness

Chicken and Poultry Times and Temperatures

CHICKEN, TURKEY, AND OTHER "WELL DONE" POULTRY

BREAST
All should be pasteurized by thickness
Medium-Rare: 137°F (58°C)
Ideal: 141°F (60.5°C)
Medium-Well: 149°F (65°C)

LEG/DRUMSTICK
Medium: 141°F (60.5°C) for 4 to 6 hours
Ideal: 148°F (64.4°C) for 4 to 6 hours
Shreddable: 165°F (73.9°C) for 8 to 12 hours

SAUSAGE
All should be pasteurized by thickness

White Meat: 141°F (60.5°C)
Dark Meat: 148°F (64.4°C)
Mixed Meat: 141°F (60.5°C)

THIGH
Medium: 141°F (60.5°C) for 4 to 6 hours
Ideal: 148°F (64.4°C) for 4 to 6 hours
Shreddable: 165°F (73.9°C) for 8 to 12 hours

WHOLE BIRD
Not recommended, but if you do, try to spatchcock it to remove the air pocket or it could harbor bacteria during the cooking process. For all temperatures it should be pasteurized by thickness.
Medium: 141°F (60.5°C)
Medium-Well: 149°F (65°C)

DUCK, GOOSE, AND "MEDIUM RARE" POULTRY

BREAST
Rare: 125°F (51.6°C) by thickness
Medium-Rare: 131°F (55°C) by thickness
Medium: 140°F (60°C) by thickness

LEG
Medium-Rare: 131°F (55°C) for 3 to 6 hours
Medium: 140°F (60°C) for 3 to 6 hours
Confit: 167°F (75°C) for 10 to 20 hours

SAUSAGE
131°F (55°C) by thickness

THIGH
Medium-Rare: 131°F (55°C) for 3 to 6 hours
Medium: 140°F (60°C) for 3 to 6 hours
Confit: 167°F (75°C) for 10 to 20 hours

WHOLE BIRD
Not recommended, but if you do, try to spatchcock it to remove the air pocket. For all temperatures it should be heated by thickness.
Medium-Rare: 131°F (55°C) for 3 to 6 hours
Medium: 140°F (60°C) for 3 to 6 hours

Eggs

The timing will change based on the size of the egg. The times below are for an average-sized American Large Grade A egg.

"RAW" PASTEURIZED EGGS
131°F (55°C) for 75 to 90 minutes

SEMI-HARD
150°F (65.6°C) for 40 to 60 minutes

SOFT BOILED / POACHED
140°F to 145°F (60°C to 62.8°C) for 40 to 60 minutes
167°F (75°C) for 13 minutes

HARD BOILED
165°F (73.9°C) for 40 to 60 minutes

Fish and Shellfish Times and Temperatures

FISH

Most fish follow the below temperatures pretty well, but different fish may be preferable at different temperatures.

GENERAL FISH TIMES

All cook times should be based on the thickness, which is about:
0.5"(13mm) thick for 14 minutes
1" (25mm) thick for 35 minutes
1.5" (38mm) thick for 1 hour 25 minutes
2" (50mm) thick for 2 hours

GENERAL FISH TEMPERATURES

Slightly Warmed: 104°F (40°C)
Firm Sashimi: 110°F (43.3°C)
Lightly Flaky and/or Firm: 120°F (48.9°C)
Very Flaky and/or Firm: 132°F (55.5°C)
Chewy: 140°F (60°C)

Warning: All of the fish you use should be high quality fish you would feel comfortable eating raw. The times and temperatures used are almost never enough to pasteurize them.

SHELLFISH

Shellfish varies greatly depending on the type you are trying to cook. Here are times and temperatures for some of the more common ones.

CRAB

132°F (55.5°C) for 30 to 60 minutes
140°F (60°C) for 30 to 60 minutes

LOBSTER

The Serious Eats guide to lobster is a great resource.
Low Temp: 115°F (46.1°C) for 20 to 40 minutes
Medium: 122°F (50°C) for 20 to 40 minutes
Ideal: 130°F (54°C) for 20 to 40 minutes
Very Firm: 140°F (60°C) for 20 to 40 minutes
Ideal Claw: 150°F (65.5°C) for 20 to 40 minutes

OCTOPUS

Slow Cook: 170°F (76.6°C) for 4 to 8 hours
Fast Cook: 180°F (82.2°C) for 2 to 4 hours

SCALLOPS

122°F (50°C) for 15 to 35 minutes
131°F (55°C) for 15 to 35 minutes

SHRIMP

Sushi-Like: 122°F (50°C) for 15 to 35 minutes
Tender: 131°F (55°C) for 15 to 35 minutes
Firm: 140°F (60°C) for 15 to 35 minutes

SQUID

Pre-Sear: 113°F (45°C) for 45 to 60 minutes
Low Heat: 138°F (58.9°C) for 2 to 4 hours
High Heat: 180°F (82.2°C) for 1 to 2 hours

Fruit and Vegetable Times and Temperatures

Almost all vegetables are cooked at 183°F (83.9°C) or higher and all entries below assume that temperature, unless otherwise stated. Hotter temperatures will cook the vegetables more quickly, but they will basically have the same texture at the end. There is also variability in a specific type of vegetable, with both their ripeness, variety, and size having an impact. So times can vary across vegetables, even of the same type.

Acorn Squash 1 to 2 hours
Apples 1 to 2 hours
Artichokes 45 to 75 minutes
Asparagus 10 to 30 minutes
Banana 10 to 15 minutes
Beet 60 to 90 minutes
Broccoli 30 to 60 minutes
Brussels Sprouts 45 to 60 minutes
Butternut Squash 45 to 60 minutes
Cabbage 60 minutes
Carrot 45 to 60 minutes
Cauliflower
   Florets 20 to 30 minutes
   For Puree 2 hours
   Stems 60 to 75 minutes
Celery Root 60 to 75 minutes
Chard 60 to 75 minutes
Cherries 15 to 25 minutes
Corn 15 to 25 minutes
Eggplant 30 to 45 minutes
Fennel 30 to 60 minutes
Golden Beets 30 to 60 minutes
Green Beans 30 to 45 minutes
Leek 30 to 60 minutes
Onion 35 to 60 minutes
Parsnip 30 to 60 minutes
Pea Pods 30 to 40 minutes
Peaches 30 to 60 minutes
Pears 25 to 60 minutes
Pineapple 167°F (75.0°C) for 45 to 60 minutes
Plums 167°F (75.0°C) for 15 to 20 minutes
Potatoes

   Small 30 to 60 minutes
   Large 60 to 120 minutes
Pumpkin 45 to 60 minutes
Radish 10 to 25 minutes
Rhubarb 141°F (60.6°C) for 25 to 45 minutes
Rutabaga 2 hours
Salsify 45 to 60 minutes
Squash
   Summer 30 to 60 minutes
   Winter 1 to 2 hours
Sunchokes 40 to 60 minutes
Sweet Potatoes
   Small 45 to 60 minutes
   Large 60 to 90 minutes
Swiss Chard 60 to 75 minutes
Turnip 45 to 60 minutes
Yams 30 to 60 minutes
Zucchini 30 to 60 minutes

Index

Image Credits

About the Author

Jason Logsdon is a passionate home cook who loves to try new things, exploring everything from sous vide and whipping siphons to blow torches, foams, spheres, and infusions. He has self published ten cookbooks that have sold, in total, more than 60,000 copies in paperback and electronic formats. His books include a best seller that hit the #1 spot on Amazon for Slow Cooking and #2 spot on Gourmet Cooking. He also runs AmazingFoodMadeEasy.com, one of the largest modernist cooking websites, and SelfPublishACookbook.com, a website dedicated to helping food bloggers successfully navigate the self-publishing process.